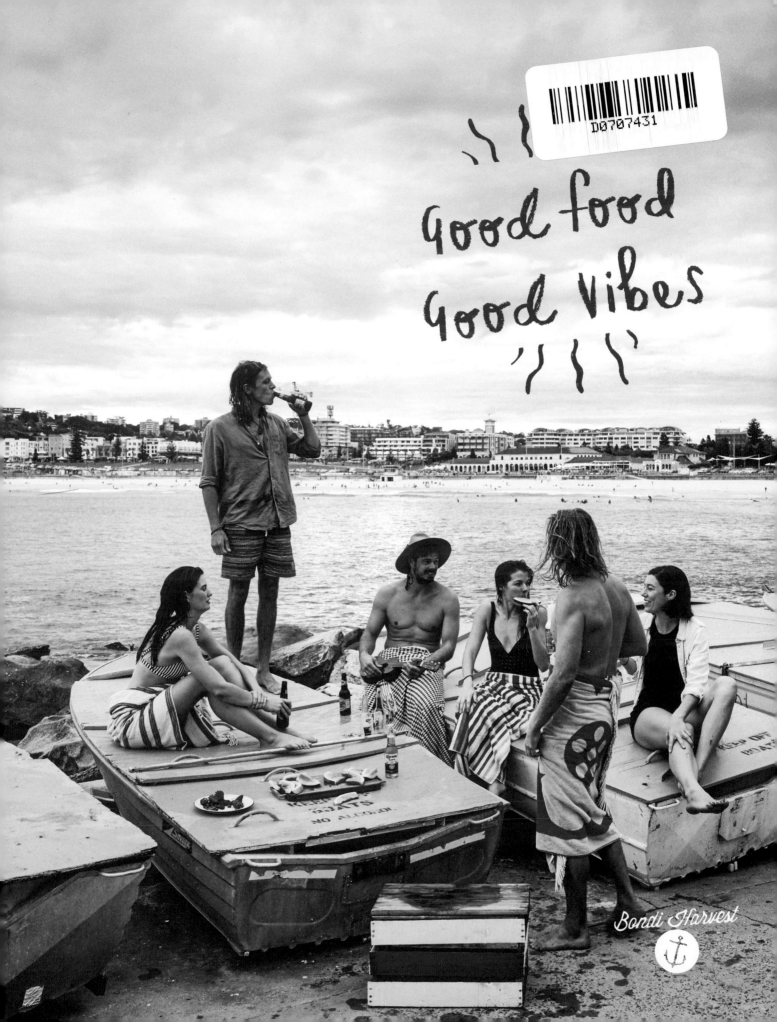

good food
good vibes

Bondi Harvest

Bondi Harvest

The Australian Wholefood Cookbook

BALANCE

GUY TURLAND & MARK ALSTON

HarperCollins*Publishers*

MAGIC MATCHA SMOOTHIE $10
100% PURE ORGANIC STONE GROUND GREEN TEA,
MANGO, MACA POWDER, CINNAMON, COCONUT MILK

BREAKFAST SMOOTHIE $10
BANANA, ALMOND MILK, DATES, CACAO NIBS,
SONOMA GRANOLA, COCONUT YOGURT, HONEY

TURMERIC LATTE $5
COCONUT MILK, ALMOND MILK, FRESH TURMERIC
UNREFINED RAPADURA SUGAR, CINNAMON.

CONTENTS

GF Gluten Free

V Vegetarian

DF Dairy Free

VE Vegan

Guy

Mark

WE ARE BACK!

And what a couple of years it has been. We've been busy making our weekly recipe videos on **bondiharvest.com**, filming our first TV series and crafting delicious wholefood menus for our Bondi Harvest cafes in the US — which brings us to the inspiration for our second Bondi Harvest cookbook.

We wanted to present to you our Bondi Harvest approach to good food and good living, and create a wholefood cookbook that reflects our journey, shares what we have learnt, and teaches, inspires and empowers you to make decisions based on your lifestyle and your own backyard — not on quick-fix diets, fads or cult food trends.

Balance is a celebration of the food we love to eat and the food we love to share with our customers, family and friends — food that we believe helps us bring balance to life. We hope it enables you to begin the journey towards finding your own balance.

When it comes to health and healthy eating, we are pretty lucky here in Australia. Our diverse climate and beautiful country provides an abundance of fresh produce and affords us an outdoor lifestyle envied around the world. Yet, even here, getting into the groove of a healthy lifestyle and finding balance can be confusing and challenging.

Trends change so rapidly and, even as professionals in the food industry, we sometimes find it difficult to separate fact from fad. But here at Bondi Harvest we work off one fundamental principle: keep it simple!

Simple means finding your balance, listening to your mind and body, and discovering what works for you. It is about making good, wholefood choices that will empower you to improve your lifestyle and achieve your personal goals.

ENJOY!
Guy & Mark

The LA Story

LA is like our second home, so it felt natural to open our first international Bondi Harvest café there – in Santa Monica to be exact. Ever since we started Bondi Harvest as a YouTube channel back in 2013, we have had a strong, supportive community in California. We think it's the beach lifestyle, the healthy living and the shared appreciation for gorgeous, fresh, seasonal produce that links us.

Opening the doors on our new café has also allowed us to expand the BH family! Sabrina, Dave, Shirley, Lupita, Vanessa and Carlo are the heart of our LA team. We are so grateful to them for being so awesome.

We are lucky to be able to work with some incredible people in the US, including Steve, Larry and Joe and all the wonderful food lovers at Tastemade, as well as some incredible food talent, including Laura Miller and Louis Tikaru. Their time, advice and friendship is invaluable.

We hope this Santa Monica café is just the beginning of our American journey. If you're ever in town, make sure you pop in and say *G'day*.

hooked

FOOD *for* good HEALTH

Being healthy means putting the right fuel into your body and having your internal engine run smoothly. This isn't a new idea. Sometime around 450 BC, Hippocrates, the father of Western medicine, said, 'Let food be thy medicine and medicine be thy food'; it was his belief that eating wholesome food is the basis for good health and – we gotta say – it makes a lot of sense.

If you are eating junk food with little or no nutrition every day, your body will not be receiving all of the nutrients it needs to function properly, and health issues might arise. The simple act of making good food choices can have the power of preventing many chronic illnesses experienced by people today.

Did you know some foods – really common foods and ingredients – have antibiotic, antifungal and anti-inflammatory properties? Now, we're not saying to stop taking your medicine (always follow your doctor's advice!), but we are simply suggesting that it makes sense to eat foods that have healing properties, such as garlic, onions and turmeric, to help combat illness. That's why many of our recipes include these ingredients. In fact, it's simple things like these that form the cornerstone of our wholefood philosophy and the Bondi Harvest Balance.

We love fuelling up on superfoods – foods rich in nutrients that are known to be beneficial for health and wellbeing – but variety is important. Individual foods have their own unique set of nutrients to meet the needs of your body, so eating a wide selection ensures that you are getting a diverse range of nutrients and vitamins.

Factoring in the seasons when planning your menu will also ensure that you derive the most health benefits from fresh and in-the-moment foods. The best rule is the fresher it is the better it is for you! You'll also save money when you buy foods that are abundantly available. Shop at local growers' markets or co-ops and talk to the sellers about what's in season.

Here are some of our favourite herbs and spices and their health benefits.

- **TURMERIC:** This spice can dramatically increase the antioxidant capacity of the body. Its active compound, curcumin, is a natural anti-inflammatory compound.

- **CINNAMON:** It can lower blood sugar levels, reduce heart disease risk factors, and has a plethora of other impressive health benefits.

- **ROSEMARY:** Its unique compounds and essential oils include rosmarinic acid and cineol, containing anti-inflammation, anti-fungal, antibacterial and antiseptic properties.

- **CAYENNE PEPPER:** One of the major benefits of cayenne pepper is the positive effect it can have on the digestive system. It can help relieve migraines and prevent blood clots.

- **FENNEL:** This vegetable is exceptionally high in fibre and vitamin C.

- **GINGER:** Gingerol is the main bioactive compound in ginger, responsible for much of its medicinal properties. It has powerful anti-inflammatory and antioxidant effects.

- **PEPPERCORN:** With strong antibacterial properties, peppercorns are a rich source of manganese, iron, potassium, vitamin C, vitamin K and dietary fibre.

- **CHAMOMILE:** This herb can help with anxiety, insomnia and muscle spasms.

Antioxidant Immune
Boost Protein Powder

Super Green
Protein Powder

Chocolate
Protein Powder

GUY'S FAVOURITE FIVE
Protein Powders

Metabolism Booster
Protein Powder

Mocha
Protein Powder

Protein powders can be a great way to supplement your daily diet. Unfortunately, many store-bought supplements are packed with nasty preservatives that are high in sugar and that in the long term can do more harm than good.

So I thought I'd share with you my five favourite homemade, healthy, vegetarian protein powders. Make them at home and be in complete control of what you put into your body.

Store your protein powders in an airtight container until you're ready to use them. All you have to do is add a few tablespoons to your favourite smoothie, frozen breakfast bowl or raw dessert recipe.

PROTEIN POWDERS

ANTIOXIDANT IMMUNE BOOST PROTEIN POWDER

(GF) (V) (DF) (VE) Makes 3 cups

160 g (5½ oz/1 cup) hemp seeds
160 g (5½ oz/1 cup) chia seeds
100 g (3½ oz/1 cup) almond meal
2 tablespoons maca powder
2 teaspoons stevia or coconut sugar (optional)
¼ teaspoon cayenne pepper
½ teaspoon ground turmeric
½ teaspoon ground cinnamon
½ teaspoon ground ginger

Place the hemp and chia seeds into a coffee or spice grinder and grind to a powder. Combine with the remaining ingredients.

Store in an airtight container in a dry place for up to 2 weeks.

METABOLISM BOOSTER PROTEIN POWDER

(GF) (V) (DF) (VE) Makes 3 cups

320 g (11¼ oz/2 cups) hemp seeds
100 g (3½ oz/1 cup) almond meal
1 tablespoon matcha (green tea) powder
1 tablespoon maca powder
2 teaspoons stevia or coconut sugar (optional)
1 teaspoon ground turmeric
½ teaspoon ground cinnamon
½ teaspoon ground ginger
½ teaspoon activated charcoal
⅓ teaspoon cayenne pepper

Place the hemp seeds into a coffee or spice grinder and grind to a powder. Combine with the remaining ingredients.

Store in an airtight container in a dry place for up to 2 weeks.

CHOCOLATE PROTEIN POWDER

(V) *Makes 5 cups*

90 g (3 oz/1 cup) rolled oats
100 g (3½ oz/1 cup) quinoa flakes
1 tablespoon cacao nibs
200 g (7 oz/2 cups) low-fat milk powder
100 g (3½ oz/1 cup) almond meal
1 tablespoon 100% raw cacao powder
2 teaspoons stevia or coconut sugar (optional)

Place the rolled oats, quinoa flakes and cacao nibs into a coffee or spice grinder and grind to a powder. Combine with the remaining ingredients.

Store in an airtight container in a dry place for up to 2 weeks.

MOCHA PROTEIN POWDER

(V) *Makes 5–6 cups*

90 g (3 oz/1 cup) rolled oats
100 g (3½ oz/1 cup) quinoa flakes
30 g (1 oz/⅓ cup) coffee beans
1 tablespoon cacao nibs
200 g (7 oz/2 cups) low-fat milk powder
100 g (3½ oz/1 cup) almond meal
2 tablespoons maca powder
2 tablespoons 100% raw cacao powder
2 teaspoons stevia or coconut sugar (optional)

Place the rolled oats, quinoa flakes, coffee beans and cacao nibs into a coffee or spice grinder and grind to a powder. Combine with the remaining ingredients.

Store in an airtight container in a dry place for up to 2 weeks.

SUPER GREEN PROTEIN POWDER

(GF) (V) (DF) (VE) *Makes 3 cups*

160 g (5½ oz/1 cup) chia seeds
40 g (1½ oz/¼ cup) flax seeds
40 g (1½ oz/¼ cup) hemp seeds
200 g (7 oz/2 cups) almond meal
3 tablespoons spirulina
1 tablespoon matcha (green tea) powder
1 tablespoon maca powder
2 teaspoons stevia or coconut sugar (optional)
¼ teaspoon ground ginger
¼ teaspoon ground cinnamon

Place the chia seeds, flax seeds and hemp seeds into a coffee or spice grinder and grind to a powder. Combine with the remaining ingredients.

Store in an airtight container in a dry place for up to 2 weeks.

FERMENTED & PICKLED

There is a good chance you have heard about the importance of gut flora (or gut health) in overall health and wellbeing. This refers to the idea that, basically, your gut does a lot more than just digest food. In fact, it is considered the largest immune system organ in the body – so you need to look after it!

The ancient practice of fermentation was used for preserving food before the time of refrigeration, but also more importantly for enhancing the nutrition profile of foods. Fermented foods are packed full with probiotics, which play an integral part in balancing the levels of good bacteria in your gut, contributing to a healthy and fully functioning digestive system.

Here's how fermented food is claimed to heal and support the body:

1. **Restores and increases gut health and digestion**
2. **Supports immune system function**
3. **Helps better absorption of nutrients from food**
4. **Detoxifies the body**
5. **Controls inflammation**
6. **Helps with food allergy and sensitivity**

What was once something you did with your granny is now something you do with your super-cool, healthy hipster mates. Fermenting and pickling your own vegetables can save you money and the results taste amazing!

For some more in-depth fermenting information, and why fermented food is so good for you, check out: www.bondiharvest.com.

KIMCHI

(GF) (DF) Makes about 1 kg (2 lb 4 oz)

1 kg (2 lb 4 oz) Chinese (napa) cabbage
  (also called wombok)
30 g (1 oz/¼ cup) + 1 tablespoon sea salt
6 cups + 2 tablespoons distilled water
8 garlic cloves, minced
1½ tablespoons finely grated fresh ginger
30 g (1 oz/⅓ cup) dried chilli flakes
1½ teaspoons white sugar
2 teaspoons Korean salted shrimp, minced (optional)
½ nori sheet, torn into small pieces
2 daikon radishes, trimmed and cut into matchsticks
1 bunch spring onions (scallions), trimmed, cut
  into 2.5 cm (1 inch) sections

Cut the cabbage in half lengthways, remove the core
then shred crossways. Place into a large mixing bowl.
Add ¼ cup salt and massage into cabbage, then add
enough distilled water to cover. Place a plate and weight
on top of the cabbage and let sit in a dark, dry place for
4 hours.

Strain and rinse the cabbage, and clean the mixing bowl
for reuse.

Combine the garlic, ginger, chilli flakes, sugar, shrimp (if
using) and nori in the mixing bowl with 2 tablespoons
of distilled water. Mix until a thick paste forms and the
sugar dissolves. Add 1 tablespoon of salt.

Add the daikon, spring onions and cabbage. Mix with the
spice paste and massage for about 5 minutes or until all
vegetables are coated in paste.

Pack into a clean 2-litre (2-quart) capacity jar. Use your
hands or a kitchen tool to press the mixture down to the
bottom of the vessel so that the juices rise to cover the
solid parts. If there aren't enough juices to cover, just top
it up with water. Seal tightly and leave to ferment out of
direct light for 3–6 days, then refrigerate.

SALT FERMENTED VEGETABLES

(GF) (V) (DF) (VE) Makes 2 kg (4 lb 8 oz)

500 g white cabbage, finely sliced
500 g carrot, finely sliced
500 g fennel, finely sliced
500 g white onion, finely sliced
30 g (1 oz/¼ cup) sea salt
1 shallot, sliced
1 teaspoon dried chilli flakes
1 garlic clove, minced
1 teaspoon coriander seeds
1 teaspoon black peppercorns
¼ teaspoon ground turmeric
1 sprig tarragon

Choose two 1-litre (34 fl oz/4 cups) wide-mouthed jars.
Use glass, plastic or ceramic – something that will not
leach chemicals into the ferment.

Wash the vegetables very well under cold water, drain
and then place into a large mixing bowl.

Add the salt, shallot, chilli flakes, garlic, coriander seeds,
peppercorns, turmeric and tarragon. Using your hands,
massage the vegetables, squeezing and pressing the
juices out and breaking down the cell walls.

Place the mixture into the jars, leaving 5 cm (2 inches)
or so of empty space at the top of the vessel. Use your
hands or a kitchen tool to press the vegetables down to
the bottom of the vessel so that the juices rise to cover
the solid parts. If there aren't enough juices to cover the
vegetables, just top them up with water.

Wrap the top of the jars with cheesecloth and seal with
a rubber band.

Leave in a dry place out of direct light for 3–6 days,
tasting every day from the third day onwards. The longer
you leave it the more the flavour will develop.

Once you're happy with the flavour, cover and store in
the fridge for up to 8 months.

KOMBUCHA

GF **V** **DF** **VE** *Makes 3 litres (105 fl oz/12cups)*

70 g (2½ oz/1 cup) black tea leaves
220 g (8 oz/1 cup) sugar
1 vanilla bean, split, seeds scraped
1 scoby (see note below)

Make a batch of sweet black tea by combining tea leaves, sugar, vanilla seeds and 3 litres (3 quarts) water in a saucepan. Bring to a simmer, then cool. Strain into a large clean jar.

Add the scoby, place a clean cloth over the top and secure with a rubber band or twine. This is to stop dust from getting in but allow gas to escape during fermentation.

Place in a dry dark place and leave to ferment for 3–5 days out of direct light.

Optional: To do a second ferment to add flavour and to carbonate the kombucha, combine 10 diced strawberries with 2 litres kombucha. Cover tightly then leave to ferment for 3 days. Strain and refrigerate.

NOTE: A scoby is the 'mother' you need to start the fermentation process. You'll have to beg, borrow or steal one from a friend who makes kombucha, or possibly ask at your local health food shop or café. When you make kombucha, a new scoby will grow underneath the old one. Use the new one for your next batch.

Scoby is an acronym - symbiotic culture of bacteria (and) yeast.

PRESERVED VINEGAR PICKLED VEGETABLES

GF **V** **DF** **VE** *Makes 500 g (1 lb 2 oz)*

250 ml (9 fl oz/1 cup) apple cider vinegar
110 g (3¾ oz/½ cup) white sugar
5 whole cloves
1 tablespoon fennel seeds
500 g (1 lb 2 oz) vegetables, sliced or chopped
   as desired

Sterilise a 1-litre (34 fl oz/4 cup) capacity mason jar and its detached lid by placing them in a large saucepan of water. Bring to the boil then let sit for 10–15 minutes. Drain.

Place the vinegar, 250 ml (9 fl oz/1 cup) water, sugar, cloves and seeds into a large saucepan. Bring to a simmer over low heat, stirring to dissolve sugar.

Place the vegetables into the pickling liquid and return to a simmer. Cook for about 7–8 minutes, or until the vegetables are tender.

Transfer vegetables and liquid into sterilised jar. Tap jar as you pour to release any air bubbles. Put lid on.

Place a saucepan of simmering water on the stove. Add jar and allow it to simmer for about 20 minutes, to create a vacuum seal.

Remove jar and place on a cloth to cool down completely, then store in a dark dry place.

NOTE: You can pickle a mixture of vegetables, or just the one type. To make pickled fennel, use 500 g (1 lb 2 oz) sliced fennel bulbs.

Whether it's to help kick the flu, for everyday health or just because they taste absolutely delicious, the right mix of herbs and spices can have some health benefits.

TEAS & ELIXIRS

ANTI-INFLAMMATORY ELIXIR

GF V DF *Serves 2–3*

½ lemon, sliced
1 cm (½ inch) piece fresh ginger
2 teaspoons honey
1 teaspoon ground turmeric
1 tablespoon coconut oil
¼ teaspoon cayenne pepper

Combine the lemon, ginger, honey, turmeric, coconut oil and cayenne pepper with 1 litre (34 fl oz) water in a saucepan. Simmer for 10 minutes, then strain.

Serve hot, or chill and drink cold later.

CHILLI, CINNAMON, CACAO NIB TEA

GF V DF *Serves 1–2*

60 g (2 oz/½ cup) cacao nibs
1 cinnamon stick
1 tablespoon honey
¼ teaspoon cayenne pepper

Combine the cacao nibs, cinnamon, honey, cayenne pepper and 500ml (17 fl oz/2 cups) water in a small saucepan.

Bring to a gentle simmer and cook for 10 minutes. Strain and serve warm.

CHILLI ELIXIR

GF V DF *Serves 2*

1 tablespoon chamomile tea leaves
1 cinnamon stick
1 teaspoon fennel seeds
2 sprigs lavender
1 sage leaf
zest of ¼ lemon, in wide strips
1 teaspoon honey

Combine all the ingredients with 500 ml (17 fl oz/ 2 cups) water in a small saucepan. Bring just to a gentle simmer, then strain. Drink hot or cold.

DETOX TEA

GF V DF *Serves 1–2*

1 tablespoon chamomile tea leaves
1 tablespoon chopped fresh ginger
1 tablespoon honey
1 lemon, sliced
4 strawberries, halved
1 sprig mint
¼ teaspoon cayenne pepper

Combine all the ingredients in a teapot. Add 500 ml (17 fl oz/2 cups) boiling water, and let steep for 10–15 minutes. Strain and serve hot.

EARTH ELIXIR

 Serves 2–3

1 cm (½ inch) piece fresh ginger
5 mm (¼ inch) piece fresh turmeric
2 coriander roots
1 lemongrass stick
1 cinnamon stick
1 parsley root
1 tablespoon honey

Combine all the ingredients with 1 litre (34 fl oz/4 cups) water in a saucepan. Bring to a simmer and cook for 15 minutes to release the flavours.

Strain and serve hot or cold.

TURMERIC CHAI

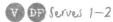 Serves 1–2

3 green cardamom pods, bruised
2 slices fresh ginger
1 cinnamon stick
¼ teaspoon fennel seeds
1 slice fresh or 1 teaspoon ground turmeric
¼ teaspoon black peppercorns
1 teaspoon black tea leaves
250 ml (9 fl oz/1 cup) milk
½ teaspoon honey (optional)

Combine the cardamom pods, ginger, cinnamon, fennel seeds, turmeric and black pepper in a dry saucepan. Cook, stirring, over medium heat for 2 minutes or until fragrant and toasted.

Add 250 ml (9 fl oz/1 cup) water and slowly bring to a simmer. Add tea leaves, milk and honey, and simmer for 30 seconds.

Strain and enjoy.

'Tea tempers the spirit, harmonises the mind, dispels lassitude and relieves fatigue, awakens the thought and prevents drowsiness.' —LU YU, The Classic Art of Tea

BALANCE TIP#1
KITCHEN RESET

Set yourself up in a healthy environment by reducing temptations and maximising good options. The best way to achieve this is through a kitchen reset.

GET RID OF THESE:

OILS
Canola oil
Sunflower oil
Fake butters

FLOUR
Bleached white flour

BREAD
White bread
White wraps
Flour tortillas

SUGARS
White sugar
Brown sugar
Icing sugar
Powdered sugar
Fake maple syrup

DRINKS
Soft drinks
Juice
Confectionery

OTHER
Table salt
Yellow cheese
Whey protein
Chips
Lollies
Sweet milk chocolate

STOCK YOUR PANTRY WITH THESE:

OILS
Olive oil
Coconut oil

GRAINS & FLOURS
Quinoa
Buckwheat
Chickpeas
Chia seeds
100% raw cacao
   powder (no sugar)
Wholemeal flour
Buckwheat flour
Rolled oats
Lentils
Farro
Polenta
Tapioca
Tapioca flour
Teff

SUGARS
Coconut sugar
Real maple syrup
Honey

VINEGARS
Apple cider vinegar
Balsamic vinegar
Red/White wine
   vinegar

SPICES
Turmeric
Cayenne pepper
Pepper
Cinnamon
Clove
Ginger powder
Chia seeds
Hemp seeds
Activated charcoal

DRINKS
Kombucha
Herbal teas

OTHER
Sea or rock salt
Hemp or pea protein

BREAKFAST

Breakfast gets your metabolism going in the morning, helping your body to create the energy it will burn up throughout the day.

With such an array of world-class produce on offer around this diverse country, we celebrate breakfast by respecting and elevating our seasonal ingredients with simple techniques that showcase them best. These recipes are designed to kick-start your day and bring balance back to your mornings.

BREAKFAST BOWLS 38

Fire up the body's engine and brain from the get-go with the right kind of fuel: real food and real flavour. In true Aussie wholefood fashion, these all-in-one breakfast bowls are an awesome way to get those body-healing ingredients into your system bright and early in the day.

CHIA SEED PUDDINGS 42

The Aztecs had it right when they introduced the humble Chia seed to the world. Chia seeds are packed with omega-3, protein, antioxidants, calcium and fibre, and can absorb eight times their own weight in liquid. This high absorption rate means that you can supercharge your breakfast with some wicked flavours.

WEEKEND BREAKFASTS 46

These recipes are designed for when you have that little bit more time to prepare a variety of morning glory wholefoods. Enjoy these with family and friends— and possibly the neighbours if they get a waft of your creation!

WAFFLES & PANCAKES 59

My all-time favourite healthy waffle recipes—for pancakes, just spoon your batter onto a frypan instead of a waffle iron—and a few delish sweet and savoury toppings to go with them. I'll show you how to make them in record time, without compromising on healthy ingredients, so you can eat them every day of the week!

JUICES & SMOOTHIES 64

Fresh juices and smoothies are a great way to get a little extra of that good stuff into your diet. These recipes are the perfect balance of greens, spices and detoxifying treats, avoiding the overly sugary fruit fads that often come in a breakfast disguise.

FROZEN BREAKFAST BOWLS 68

Hot Aussie summer mornings call for the perfect chilled wholefood breakfast bowl designed to turbo-charge the body in the morning and 'detox' from the night before. – YEW!

BREAKFAST BOWLS

KOMBUCHA BIRCHER

Ⓥ Serves 5–6

500 g (1 lb 2 oz) quinoa flakes or rolled oats
120 g (4 oz/1 cup) sultanas (golden raisins)
1 tablespoon chai tea leaves
½ teaspoon fresh thyme leaves, chopped
500 ml (17 fl oz/2 cups) kombucha (page 27)
520 g (1 lb 2½ oz/2 cups) natural yoghurt
2 tablespoons slivered almonds
2 tablespoons pepitas (pumpkin seeds)
145 g (5½ oz/1 cup) fresh berries
honey, to drizzle
edible flowers (optional)

Combine the quinoa flakes or oats, sultanas, chai tea leaves, thyme and kombucha in a bowl. Place into the fridge for at least 30 minutes (but ideally overnight) to soak.

To serve, stir the yoghurt through the mixture. Top with almonds, pepitas, berries, a drizzle of honey and a sprinkle of edible flowers (if using).

TIMESAVING HACK: Divide between recycled jars, ready to grab and go for work, or to feed the family in the morning.

HEALTHY BLACK FOREST BROWN RICE BREAKFAST PUDDING

ⒼⒻ Ⓥ Serves 3–4

1 cup (200 g/7 oz) brown rice
1 cup (250 ml/9 fl oz) almond, coconut
  or cow's milk
1 vanilla bean, split, seeds scraped
1 teaspoon ground cinnamon (or 1 cinnamon stick)
finely grated zest of 1 lemon
2 bananas, mashed
2 teaspoons honey
2 tablespoons 100% raw cacao powder
70 g (2½ oz/½ cup) raspberries (frozen or fresh)
½ cup (25 g/¾ oz) coconut flakes, toasted
1 tablespoon mixed nuts

Place the rice into a saucepan with 375 ml (13 fl oz/1 ½ cups) water. Bring to the boil over high heat. Cover, reduce the heat to low and simmer for 20 minutes. Remove from the heat and sit, covered, for 10 minutes. Drain any excess liquid.

Mix the cooked rice, milk, vanilla seeds, cinnamon and lemon zest in a saucepan. Cook over medium heat for 10 minutes, stirring constantly, until the mixture has a porridge consistency.

Combine the banana, honey and cacao in a bowl and mix until smooth. Fold the porridge mixture through.

Serve warm, topped with the berries, coconut and nuts.

NOTE: You can use buckwheat instead of brown rice if you like.

CAULIFLOWER RICE RAINBOW BREAKFAST BOWL

GF V Serves 4

1 garlic clove
100 ml (3½ fl oz) olive oil
50 g (1¾ oz) rocket (arugula)
½ bunch basil, leaves picked
70 g (2½ oz) almonds
70 g (2½ oz) parmesan cheese, grated
finely grated zest and juice of 1 lemon
1 cauliflower, florets only
½ cup pickled fennel (see Preserved Vinegar
  Pickled Vegetables, page 27)
1 cup turmeric quinoa (page 215)
1 avocado, quartered and sliced
4 fried or soft boiled eggs
1 tablespoon pistachio dukkah (page 218)

Put the garlic and olive oil into a mortar and pestle or food processor and season with salt and pepper. Grind to a smooth paste. Add the rocket, basil, almonds, parmesan and lemon juice. Grind to make a pesto.

Place the cauliflower florets into a food processor and process to a fine rice-like consistency. Mix in the lemon zest.

Mix 2 teaspoons of the pesto with 1 cup of cauliflower rice and season with salt and pepper.

Divide the pesto cauliflower rice, pickled fennel, avocado and turmeric quinoa between bowls. Top each with an egg, and sprinkle with dukkah.

TIMESAVING HACK: Keep leftover pesto and cauliflower rice in the fridge for up to 5 days. It's great to have ready to eat in a salad or quick breakfast.

QUINOA NASI GORENG

DF Serves 3-4

1 tablespoon coconut oil
½ bunch spring onions (scallions), chopped
2 garlic cloves, finely chopped
2 small red chillies, finely chopped
4 shallots, chopped
200 g (7 oz) chicken (breast or thigh fillet),
  coarsely chopped
3 prawns (shrimp), cleaned and diced (optional)
⅓ teaspoon shrimp paste (optional)
240 g (8½ oz/2 cups) cooked quinoa
1 tablespoon kecap manis
1 cucumber, diced
2 tomatoes, diced
3-4 fried eggs

Heat the coconut oil in a large frying pan over medium-high heat. Add the spring onions, garlic, chilli and shallots. Cook, stirring, for 1-2 minutes or until fragrant.

Add the chicken and prawns (if using). Cook, stirring, for about 2 minutes to seal. Add the shrimp paste, quinoa and kecap manis. Cook, stirring, until the chicken is cooked through.

Remove from heat and stir the cucumber and tomatoes through. Serve with a fried egg on top.

YEWW!

Fun Fact: Did you know Chia seeds first hit the market as terracotta figurines called Chia Pets? Moistened Chia seeds are applied to the grooved terracotta which has been shaped as a head or body. The seeds then sprout over a couple of weeks to produce the 'hair' or 'fur' of the figurine.

CHIA SEED PUDDINGS

BERRY SPLICE, VANILLA & COCONUT CHIA SEED PUDDING

(GF) (V) (DF) (VE) *Serves 4—5*

500 ml (17 fl oz/2 cups) coconut milk
60 ml (2 fl oz/¼ cup) maple syrup
½ teaspoon vanilla extract (or ½ vanilla bean, split, seeds scraped)
80 g (2¾ oz/½ cup) chia seeds
2 tablespoons coconut flakes, toasted (optional)

BERRY COMPOTE

145 g (5½ oz/1 cup) mixed frozen berries (or fresh)
1 tablespoon maple syrup
finely grated zest and juice of 1 lemon
1 teaspoon finely grated fresh ginger

To make the berry compote, combine the berries, maple syrup, lemon zest, juice and ginger in a saucepan over low heat. Cook for 10 minutes, or until berries have collapsed to a jammy consistency and the flavours have come together. Transfer to a bowl and leave to cool.

For the pudding, mix the coconut milk, maple syrup and vanilla extract or seeds in a mixing bowl. Add the chia seeds and mix well. Cover and place into the fridge for at least 3 hours (but ideally overnight) to thicken.

Layer berry compote and chia pudding into bowls, or into glass jars ready to take to work, topped with toasted coconut (if using).

NOTE: Berry compote will keep for up to 1 week in the fridge.

PB&J CHIA SEED PUDDING

(GF) (V) *Serves 4—5*

375 ml (13 fl oz/1½ cups) almond or cow's milk
2 tablespoons peanut butter (page 210)
55 g (1¾ oz/⅓ cup) chia seeds
¼ cup healthy jam (page 212)
Bondi Harvest granola (page 214), optional

Put the milk and peanut butter into a food processor or blender and blend until smooth.

Pour into a mixing bowl then add the chia seeds and mix well. Place into the fridge for at least 3 hours (but ideally overnight) to thicken.

Layer jam and puddings into bowls, or in glass jars ready to take to work, topped with some granola, if using.

HEALTHY CHOCOLATE HAZELNUT PUDDING

(GF) (V) (DF) (VE) *Serves 4—5*

310 ml (10½ fl oz/1¼ cups) coconut milk
1 tablespoon hazelnut spread (page 210)
1 tablespoon maple syrup
pinch sea salt
25 g (¾ oz/¼ cup) 100% raw cacao powder
40 g (1½ oz/¼ cup) chia seeds
65 g (2¼ oz/½ cup) hazelnuts, toasted and chopped

Put the coconut milk, hazelnut spread, maple syrup, sea salt and cacao powder into a food processor or blender and blend until smooth.

Pour into a mixing bowl then add the chia seeds and mix well. Place into the fridge for at least 3 hours (but ideally overnight) to thicken.

Serve in bowls, or in glass jars ready to take to work, sprinkled with chopped hazelnuts.

GREEN MACHINE CHIA SEED PUDDING

(GF) (V) (DF) *Serves 4—5*

⅓ avocado, flesh scooped out
1 teaspoon matcha powder
1 banana
2 tablespoons honey (or 1 tablespoon agave syrup)
375 ml (12 fl oz/1½ cups) coconut water
55 g (1¾ oz/⅓ cup) chia seeds
65 g (2¼ oz/½ cup) strawberries, quartered
1 tablespoon chopped mint leaves

Put the avocado, matcha powder, banana, honey and coconut water into a food processor or blender and blend until smooth.

Pour into a mixing bowl then add the chia seeds and mix well. Place into the fridge for at least 3 hours (but ideally overnight) to thicken.

Serve in bowls, or in glass jars ready to take to work, topped with strawberries and chopped mint.

CHILLI CHOC CHIA SEED PUDDING

(GF) (V) (DF) (VE) *Serves 4—5*

310 ml (10½ fl oz/1¼ cups) coconut milk
1 tablespoon maple syrup
25 g (¾ oz/¼ cup) 100% raw cacao powder
1 teaspoon cayenne pepper
1 tablespoon cocoa nibs
pinch sea salt
40 g (1½ oz/¼ cup) chia seeds

Combine the coconut milk, maple syrup, cacao powder, cayenne pepper, cocoa nibs and salt in a mixing bowl.

Add the chia seeds and mix well. Place into the fridge for at least 3 hours (but ideally overnight) to thicken.

Serve in bowls, or in glass jars ready to take to work.

Healthy
Chocolate Hazelnut
Pudding

Berry Splice
Vanilla & Coconut
Chia Seed Pudding

Chilli Choc
Chia Seed
Pudding

PB&J Chia
Seed Pudding

CHAI-SPICED HOT SMOKED SALMON

GF DF *Serves 5—6*

CURING MIX

1 cinnamon stick

1 star anise

1 black peppercorn

1 teaspoon ground ginger

1 clove

1 teaspoon ground nutmeg

250 g (9 oz) salt

250 g (9 oz) sugar

finely grated zest of 1 orange

SMOKED SALMON

2 cups smoking woodchips, soaked in water for 30 minutes

1.5 kg salmon fillet, skin on

SALAD

250 ml (9 fl oz/1 cup) apple cider vinegar

2 teaspoons honey

1 cucumber, cut into 1 cm (½ inch) dice

2 baby cos (romaine) lettuces

3 avocados, chopped

1 bunch mint, leaves picked

1 bunch parsley, leaves picked

6 lemon wedges

Preheat oven to 175°C (340°F).

To make the curing mix, place the spices onto a baking tray and bake in the oven for 10 minutes, until toasted and fragrant. Use a mortar and pestle or food processor to grind the spices to a coarse mixture. Combine the spice mixture with the salt, sugar and orange zest.

To hot-smoke the salmon, drain the soaked woodchips and place them in the base of a smoker. Spread 1 cup of the curing mix over the skinless side of the salmon, and place skin side down on the rack above the woodchips.

Heat the smoker on high heat for about 5 minutes, until it begins to smoke. Reduce the heat to low and smoke the salmon for 30 minutes. Turn off the heat and rest the salmon for 3–5 minutes before eating.

For the salad, mix the vinegar and honey in a bowl. Add the cucumber and leave for 10 minutes, to pickle.

Separate the lettuce into whole leaves to use as cups and place onto a serving board with the avocado, herbs and lemon wedges.

Serve whole salmon on a board or still in smoking tray. Pull off chunks of salmon and serve in lettuce cups with cucumber, herbs, avocado and lemon.

NOTE: Store the curing mix, without the orange zest, in an airtight container for up to 1 month.

BAKED HASSELBACK GRANOLA CRUMBLE

GF V Serves 4—5

3 apples or pears, halved

1 tablespoon coconut oil

1 teaspoon ground cinnamon

3 cups Bondi Harvest granola (page 214)

260 g (9¼ oz/1 cup) Greek or homemade yoghurt (page 216)

2 teaspoons honey or maple syrup

145g (5½ oz/1 cup) fresh mixed berries (optional)

Preheat the oven to 180°C (350°F) and line a rimmed baking tray with baking paper.

Place the apples or pears cut side down on a chopping board. Cut slices 5 mm apart, but not all the way through. Stop just before you cut through the bottom to keep the slices connected.

Place onto the baking tray flat side down. Brush with coconut oil then sprinkle with cinnamon. Bake for 15 minutes or until tender.

Remove tray from the oven and sprinkle granola over and around the baked fruit. Bake for another 10 minutes to finish.

Serve topped with dollops of yoghurt, a drizzle of honey and the berries (if using).

EGGS IN STUFFED PEPPERS

GF *Serves 5*

60 g (2 oz) butter

2 red onions, finely sliced

2 garlic cloves, minced

2 small red chillies, finely chopped

520 g (1 lb 2½ oz/2 cups) ricotta

180 g (6 oz/1 cup) cooked chickpeas

½ cup coriander (cilantro) leaves, chopped

finely grated zest of 2 lemons
   (reserve the lemons)

1 tablespoon ground cumin

30 g (1 oz/3 tablespoons) sultanas
   (golden raisins)

300 g (10½ oz) chai-spiced hot smoked
   salmon, flaked (page 47)

3 cups spinach leaves, blanched and chopped

5 large red capsicums (peppers),
   halved lengthways

500 ml (17 fl oz/2 cups) passata (page 126)

10 eggs

520 g (1 lb 2½ oz/2 cups) Greek or
   homemade yoghurt (page 216)

2 teaspoons smoked paprika

coriander (cilantro) leaves, to serve

150 g (5½ oz/1 cup) pine nuts

Preheat oven to 200°C (400°F).

Melt the butter in a frying pan over medium heat. Add the onion, garlic and chillies and cook, stirring occasionally, until soft. Cool.

Place the onion mixture into a large mixing bowl with the ricotta, chickpeas, coriander, lemon zest, cumin, sultanas, salmon and spinach. Season with salt and mix until evenly combined. Spoon into the capsicum halves (they should be about half full).

Spread the passata into the base of a large roasting pan. Arrange the capsicums into the pan, cut side up. Bake for 10–15 minutes, until hot and semi-caramelised.

Take the tray out of the oven and squeeze lemon juice over the capsicums. Crack one egg into each stuffed capsicum. Bake for another 10–15 minutes, until the eggs are set.

Serve with a dollop of yoghurt, and sprinkle with paprika, coriander and pine nuts.

NOTE: Use chopped kale instead of spinach if you like.

OVER-SIZED POTATO ROSTI BREAKFAST

GF *Serves 5*

500 g (1 lb 2 oz) potato, grated or spiralled
2 teaspoons sea salt
1 teaspoon cracked pepper
1 teaspoon fennel seeds
finely grated zest of 1 lemon
1 small red chilli, finely chopped
2 garlic cloves, minced
1 teaspoon ground turmeric
1 tablespoon finely chopped parsley leaves
2 teaspoons finely grated parmesan cheese
60 ml (2 fl oz/¼ cup) olive oil
5 tablespoons Greek or homemade yoghurt
  (page 216)
5 eggs, fried
¼ cup pistachio dukkah (page 218)

Mix the potato and sea salt in a large bowl and let sit for at least 1 hour to draw out the excess moisture.

Preheat oven to 180°C (350°F)

Place the potato into a strainer and squeeze to remove liquid. Transfer to a clean bowl and add pepper, fennel seeds, lemon zest, chilli, garlic, turmeric, parsley and parmesan. Mix well.

Heat a 20 cm (8 inch) heavy-based ovenproof frying pan over medium-high heat. Add the olive oil, then add the potato mixture one handful at a time, stirring to evaporate any excess liquid between each addition.

When all the potato has been added, pat into a flat rosti shape. Place in the oven for 15 minutes until the base is coloured, then carefully flip and bake for another 5–10 minutes. Turn out onto a chopping board.

Cut into wedges and top with yoghurt, fried eggs and dukkah.

MEXICAN SALSA VERDE EGGS

(V) Serves 4—5

1 cup washed and sliced kale

4–5 eggs

3 tablespoons ricotta, crumbled

1 tablespoon pomegranate seeds

roughly crushed macadamia nuts, to taste

fresh crusty bread or tortillas, to serve

MEXICAN SALSA VERDE

10 tomatillos, husked

½ red onion, sliced

1 garlic clove, minced

2 jalapenos, coarsely chopped

½ teaspoon finely grated fresh ginger

1 bunch coriander (cilantro), leaves picked

finely grated zest and juice of 2 limes

To make the salsa verde, preheat the oven to 180°C (350°F). Place tomatillos onto a baking tray and bake for 10 minutes. Add the onion and bake for a further 20 minutes, until tender and lightly coloured.

Transfer the hot tomatillos and onions to a food processor or blender and add the garlic, jalapenos, ginger, coriander (reserve 1 tablespoon for serving), lime zest and juice. Process or blend until smooth. Season with salt and pepper.

Mix 2 cups salsa verde with the kale in a shallow 25 cm (10 inch) frying pan. Crack the eggs one by one into the pan.

Place the frying pan over medium heat and cook for 20–25 minutes, until the sauce is hot and the egg whites are cooked but yolks are still soft.

Scatter with the reserved coriander, ricotta, pomegranate seeds and macadamia nuts. Serve with fresh crusty bread or tortillas.

NOTE: Salsa verde will keep in the fridge for up to 2 weeks.

WAFFLES & PANCAKES

SOURDOUGH WAFFLES

Ⓥ *Makes 10*

OVERNIGHT SPONGE

1 cup sourdough starter (page 213)
250 ml (9 fl oz/1 cup) buttermilk
150 g (5½ oz/1 cup) plain (all-purpose) or rye flour
1 tablespoon coconut sugar or brown sugar

BATTER

1 egg, lightly beaten
120 g (4 oz) butter, melted or 125 ml (4 fl oz/½ cup) coconut oil
1 vanilla bean, split, seeds scraped
finely grated zest of 1 lemon
1 teaspoon bicarbonate of soda (baking soda)
½ teaspoon sea salt

To make the overnight sponge, mix the sourdough starter, buttermilk, flour and sugar in a mixing bowl until combined. Cover with plastic wrap and let sit out overnight, or for 12 hours.

For the waffles, mix the egg, butter (or coconut oil), vanilla seeds, lemon zest and bicarb in a bowl. Add the overnight sponge and salt, and mix until combined.

Grease and preheat a waffle iron. Pour about ¼ cup of the batter into the waffle iron and cook for 4–5 minutes, until golden brown. Repeat with remaining batter.

NOTE: These waffles are perfect for both sweet and savoury toppings.

ZUCCHINI BACON WAFFLES

Serves 3—4

smashed pea salad (page 63)
3–4 poached eggs (optional)

WAFFLES

150 g (5½ oz) grated zucchini
2 eggs, lightly beaten
50 g (1¾ oz) grated parmesan cheese
1 tablespoon chopped mint leaves
35 g (1¼ oz/¼ cup) self-raising flour
25 g (¾ oz) bacon, finely chopped (optional)
½ onion, finely chopped

To make the waffles, combine all the ingredients in a bowl. Grease and preheat a waffle iron.

Pour ¼ cup of the batter into the waffle iron and cook for 4–5 minutes, until golden brown. Repeat with remaining batter.

Serve topped with smashed pea salad and poached eggs (if using).

RAINBOW BOWL WAFFLES

Ⓥ Serves 4

smashed pea salad (page 63)

1 avocado, cut into quarters

4 poached eggs (optional)

WAFFLES

150 g (5½ oz) combined cauliflower rice,
corn kernels, grated beetroot and grated zucchini

2 eggs, lightly beaten

50 g (1¾ oz) grated parmesan cheese

1 tablespoon chopped mint leaves

35 g (1¼ oz/¼ cup) self-raising flour

25 g (¾ oz) salt fermented vegetables, finely chopped, optional (page 26)

½ onion, finely chopped

To make the waffles, combine all the ingredients in a bowl. Grease and preheat a waffle iron.

Pour ¼ cup of the batter into the waffle iron and cook for 4–5 minutes, until golden brown. Repeat with remaining batter.

Serve topped with smashed pea salad, avocado and poached eggs (if using). Season with freshly ground black pepper.

VANILLA COCONUT & LEMON RIND WAFFLE

Ⓥ Serves 4–6

300 g (10½ oz/2 cups) plain (all-purpose) flour

1 tablespoon baking powder

½ teaspoon sea salt

35 g (1¼ oz/ ¼ cup) coconut or brown sugar

2 eggs, separated

500 ml (17 fl oz/2 cups) coconut milk

125 ml (4 fl oz/½ cup) coconut oil

finely grated zest of 1 lemon

1 vanilla bean, split, seeds scraped

Sift the flour, baking powder, salt and sugar into a bowl. Mix the egg yolks with the milk, oil, zest and vanilla seeds. Add the dry ingredients and mix well.

Beat the egg whites until firm peaks form. Fold gently through the flour mixture. Grease and preheat a waffle iron.

Pour ¼ cup of the batter into the waffle iron and cook for 4-5 minutes, until golden. Repeat with remaining batter. Serve with your favourite waffle topping.

HIGH-PROTEIN PANCAKES

(V) Serves 4–5

2 tablespoons coconut or olive oil, for cooking
waffle toppings, to serve (page 63)

DRY MIX

150 g (5½ oz/1½ cups) almond meal
2 tablespoons pea or hemp protein powder
½ teaspoon baking powder
¼ teaspoon cayenne pepper
1 tablespoon 100% raw cacao powder

WET MIX

250 ml (9 fl oz/1 cup) milk or water
3 eggs, lightly beaten
1 tablespoon honey or maple syrup

Combine all the dry mix ingredients in an airtight
jar or plastic container, leaving about 4 cm (1½
inches) of space under the lid.

When you are ready to make pancakes, add the wet
mix ingredients. Close the lid tightly and shake until
combined and smooth.

Heat the oil in a frying pan over medium heat. Add
the pancake mix (enough for desired size) to the
pan, and cook for 2–3 minutes, until bubbles start
to form and the rim of the pancake looks cooked.

Carefully flip and cook for 1 minute, until pancake
is cooked through and coloured beautifully. Repeat
with remaining mixture.

Serve with your favourite topping.

NOTE: You can use any type of milk, such as
coconut, almond, rice or cow's. The dry mixture will
keep for up to 1 year in an airtight container. Once
mixed with the wet ingredients, it will keep for up to
5 days in the fridge. The cooked pancakes will keep
for up to 5 days in the fridge.

TWO-INGREDIENT PANCAKES

(GF) (V)

Makes 8 small or
1–2 large pancakes

1 ripe banana
1 egg
waffle toppings, to serve (page 63)

FLAVOUR OPTIONS

CHOC CHILLI PANCAKES

1 teaspoon 100% raw cacao powder
⅛ teaspoon cayenne pepper

GINGER NINJA PANCAKES

½ teaspoon ground turmeric
¼ teaspoon finely grated fresh ginger
½ teaspoon honey

SUPERFOOD PANCAKES

½ teaspoon ground cinnamon
¼ teaspoon chia seeds
¼ teaspoon flax seeds
¼ teaspoon hemp seeds
¼ teaspoon maple syrup

Use a fork to mash the banana in a mixing bowl,
then add the egg and mix well. Add any of the
flavour options if you like, or leave plain.

Heat a non-stick frying pan over medium heat. Add
the pancake mix (enough to make the size you like)
to the pan and cook for 1–2 minutes, until bubbles
start to form and the base begins to colour.
Carefully flip and cook for about 30 seconds.
Repeat with remaining mixture.

Serve hot with your favourite topping.

WAFFLE & PANCAKE TOPPINGS

BACON, MAPLE & AVOCADO SALAD

GF **DF** Serves 3—4

3 strips bacon, grilled
1 avocado, sliced
1 tablespoon maple syrup

While the bacon is still warm mix with the avocado and maple syrup. Serve on top of waffles.

ROCKMELON & MINT SALAD

GF **V** Serves 4—5

½ rockmelon, sliced into fine ribbons
2 mango cheeks, sliced into fine ribbons
½ cup mint leaves, chopped
70 g (2½ oz/½ cup) pistachios, toasted and sliced
2 lemon myrtle leaves or kaffir lime leaves, finely sliced
2 tablespoons honey
juice of 1 orange
coconut yoghurt, to serve

In a mixing bowl, mix the rockmelon, mango, mint, pistachios and lemon myrtle. Drizzle with the honey and orange juice and turn to coat.

Serve on top of waffles with coconut yoghurt.

SMASHED PEA SALAD

GF Serves 3—4

130 g (4½ oz/1 cup) green peas, cooked
65 g (2¼ oz/¼ cup) ricotta
65 g (2¼ oz/¼ cup) goat's cheese
¼ small red chilli, finely chopped
1 tablespoon dill leaves
1 tablespoon finely chopped mint leaves
4 slices smoked salmon (optional)

Place the peas into a mixing bowl and, using your hands or a fork, break up into a coarse mash. Mix in the ricotta, goat's cheese, chilli, dill and mint. Season with salt and pepper.

Serve on top of waffles with smoked salmon (if using).

SWEET AVOCADO & MINT MOUSSE

GF **V** **DF** Serves 3—4

2 avocados
½ teaspoon matcha powder
1½ tablespoons coconut oil
finely grated zest and juice of 1 lemon
finely grated zest of 1 lime
2 tablespoons chopped mint
1½ tablespoons honey or maple syrup

Put all the ingredients into a food processor and use the pulse button to process in short bursts until combined. Don't over process or the heat will discolour the purée.

Transfer to a bowl and refrigerate for 20 minutes to set.

CARIBBEAN RUM & COCONUT CARAMELISED PINEAPPLE

GF **V** **DF** **VE** Serves 3—4

340 g (12 oz/2 cups) peeled, cored and diced pineapple
2 tablespoons spiced rum
1 tablespoon coconut sugar
1 teaspoon finely grated fresh ginger
2 sprigs thyme, leaves picked
2 tablespoons coconut flakes

Add the pineapple to a hot frying pan and cook over medium-high heat until tender and caramelised. Meanwhile, mix the rum, sugar, ginger and thyme.

When the pineapple is ready, add to the rum mixture and leave to marinate for 2 minutes.

Spoon over waffles and garnish with toasted coconut.

DRINK The RAINBOW

JUICES & SMOOTHIES

Drink the Rainbow!

RED

Red fruits and veggies—such as beetroots, cherries and cranberries—are packed with phytonutrients that are believed to help prevent heart disease, prostate cancer and macular degeneration.

ORANGE & YELLOW

The gorgeous colour of carrot, mango or orange comes from carotene and carotenoids. These phytochemicals are converted into the powerful antioxidant vitamin A. Vitamin A is essential for a healthy immune system, eyes, skin and heart.

BLUE & PURPLE

Bursting with vitamin C and antioxidant, fruits and veggies such as blueberries, acai and eggplant can protect the body and reduce the risk of high blood pressure, boost the immune system and fight inflammation.

GREEN

Eat your greens, people! Green veggies and fruits are known to be among the most nutrient-dense foods. They're packed with fibre, vitamins and minerals. The epic green colour comes from the powerful antioxidant chlorophyll. The darker the green the more chlorophyll and antioxidants there are to protect our body's cells and immune system.

KOMBUCHA KICK

GF V DF VE Serves 1–2

215 g (7½ oz/1½ cups) mixed berries
100 ml (3½ fl oz) kombucha (page 27)
1 sprig thyme, leaves picked
100 ml (3½ fl oz) orange juice
1 tablespoon maple syrup
1 tablespoon chia seeds
1 tablespoon slivered macadamias
2 teaspoons goji berries

Place the berries, kombucha, thyme leaves, juice and maple syrup into a high-powered blender and blitz until smooth.

Serve cold, topped with chia seeds, macadamias and goji berries.

PEANUT BUTTER BOMB

GF V DF VE Serves 1–2

200 ml (7 fl oz) almond milk
2 tablespoons maple syrup
2 tablespoons 100% raw cacao powder
1 tablespoon peanut butter (page 210)
2 frozen peeled and chopped bananas
½ cup ice cubes
1 tablespoon dried bananas
1 tablespoon cocoa nibs

Place the milk, maple syrup, cacao powder, peanut butter, bananas and ice cubes into a high-powered blender and blitz until smooth.

Serve cold, topped with dried bananas and cocoa nibs.

CHOCOLATE CASHEW SHAKE

GF V DF Serves 1–2

250 ml (9 fl oz/1 cup) coconut water
75 g (2½ oz/½ cup) cashews
2 teaspoons 100% raw cacao powder
1 teaspoon honey
1 teaspoon vanilla essence

Place all ingredients into a high-powered blender and blitz until smooth. Serve cold.

MANGO, MINT, TURMERIC & CAYENNE PEPPER LASSI

(GF) (V) Serves 1–3

390 g (13½ oz/1½ cups) coconut yoghurt
300 g (10½ oz/1½ cups) chopped mango flesh
1 tablespoon honey or maple syrup
½ teaspoon ground turmeric
¼ teaspoon cayenne pepper
6 spearmint leaves

Place all ingredients into a high-powered blender and blitz until smooth. Serve cold.

ON THE GREEN

(GF) (V) (DF) (VE) Serves 1–2

200 g (7 oz/1 cup) mango flesh
1 cup chopped kale
1 cup chopped spinach
90 ml (3 fl oz) coconut water
60 ml (2 fl oz/¼ cup) apple juice
30 ml (1 fl oz) lemon juice
1 tablespoon maple syrup
1 teaspoon each hemp seeds, flaxseeds, toasted shredded coconut

Place the mango, kale, spinach, coconut water, juices and maple syrup into a high-powered blender and blitz until smooth.

Serve cold, topped with seeds and coconut.

DETOX

(GF) (V) (DF) (VE) Serves 1

1 lemon, quartered
1 cm (½ inch) piece ginger
80g (2¾ oz/½ cup) chopped beetroot (beet)
2 apples
3 sprigs parsley
1 teaspoon activated charcoal
½ teaspoon ground turmeric

Push the lemon, ginger, beetroot, apples and parsley though a juicer. Pour into a glass and stir in the activated charcoal and turmeric.

DIGESTIVE DELIGHT

(GF) (V) (DF) (VE) Serves 1

1 pear
2 tablespoons blueberries
¼ fennel bulb
1 lemon, quartered
½ teaspoon finely grated fresh ginger
250 ml (9 fl oz) 1 cup coconut water
½ teaspoon activated charcoal

Push the pear, blueberries, fennel, lemon and ginger through a juicer. Pour into a glass and add the coconut water and activated charcoal.

VIRUS NINJA

(GF) (V) (DF) Serves 1

¼ pear
½ lemon
2 cm (¾ inch) piece ginger
60 ml (2 fl oz/¼ cup) black tea
1 tablespoon honey
pinch thyme leaves

Push the pear, lemon and ginger through a juicer. Combine with the tea, honey, thyme and 125 ml (4 fl oz/½ cup) water.

GREEN ASS KICK

(GF) (V) (DF) (VE) Serves 1

½ lemon
¼ tomato
¼ apple
1 cm (½ inch) piece cucumber
1 cm (½ inch) piece ginger
3 spinach leaves
½ teaspoon cayenne pepper
½ teaspoon olive oil

Push the lemon, tomato, apple, cucumber, ginger and spinach through a juicer. Mix with cayenne pepper, olive oil and 60 ml (2 fl oz/¼ cup) water.

Detox Green
Bowl

Antioxidant
Bowl

Post-Workout
Protein Bowl

Kombucha
Bowl

FROZEN BOWLS

ANTIOXIDANT BOWL

(GF) (V) (DF) (VE) *Serves 2–3*

150 g (5½ oz/1 cup) frozen acai pulp
1 frozen, peeled and chopped banana
1 tablespoon blueberries
1 tablespoon chia seeds
1 teaspoon hemp seeds
1 tablespoon goji berries
¼ teaspoon ground cinnamon
375 ml (13 fl oz/1½ cups) coconut water
1 teaspoon activated charcoal
1 teaspoon slivered almonds
1 teaspoon cocoa nibs

Place the acai, banana, blueberries, chia seeds, hemp seeds, goji berries, cinnamon and coconut water into a high-powered blender and blend until thick and smooth.

Pour into bowls and garnish with activated charcoal, slivered almonds and cocoa nibs.

DETOX GREEN BOWL

(GF) (V) (DF) (VE) *Serves 2–3*

1 avocado, flesh scooped out
1 frozen peeled and chopped banana
finely grated zest of 1 lemon
½ teaspoon finely grated fresh ginger
1 cup spinach leaves
10 mint leaves
2 tablespoons maple syrup
250 ml (9 fl oz/1 cup) coconut water
1 tablespoon goji berries
1 tablespoon flaxseeds
1 tablespoon fresh berries
1 green apple, sliced
1 kiwi fruit, sliced

Place the avocado, banana, lemon zest, ginger, spinach leaves, mint, maple syrup and half the coconut water into a blender. Blend on high, slowly adding the remaining coconut water, until thick and smooth.

Pour into bowls and garnish with berries, flaxseeds, apple and kiwi fruit.

POST-WORKOUT PROTEIN BOWL

(V) (DF) Serves 2–3

1 tablespoon rolled oats

2 tablespoons protein powder

2 frozen bananas, peeled and chopped

45 g (1½ oz/⅓ cup) macadamia nuts

½ vanilla bean, split, seeds scraped

1 tablespoon honey or maple syrup

500 ml (17 fl oz/2 cups) coconut water

1 tablespoon almonds

1 cup Bondi Harvest granola (page 214)

1 banana, sliced

1 teaspoon cocoa nibs

Place the oats, protein powder, bananas, macadamias, vanilla seeds and maple syrup into a blender with half the coconut water. Blend on high, then slowly add remaining coconut water until mixture is thick and smooth.

Garnish with almonds, granola, banana and cocoa nibs.

FROZEN BERRY & KOMBUCHA BOWL

(GF) (V) (DF) (VE) Serves 2–3

145 g (5½ oz/1 cup) mixed frozen berries

3 Medjool dates, pitted

1–2 frozen, peeled and chopped bananas

2 teaspoons coconut oil

1 tablespoon chia seeds

1 teaspoon macadamia nuts

250 ml (9 fl oz/1 cup) kombucha (page 27)

1 teaspoon cocoa nibs

1 teaspoon hemp seeds

2 tablespoons fresh berries

1 small handful microherbs (optional)

Place the berries, dates, bananas, coconut oil, chia seeds, macadamia nuts and kombucha into a blender. Blend on high, until mixture is thick and smooth.

If it's a little runny, add ice cubes and blend again. Garnish with fresh berries, hemp seeds and microherbs (if using).

BH SMART TIP: Not all hydration comes from water. Some fruits and vegetables are actually twice as hydrating as water, because they also contain hydrating salts, minerals and sugars. So stock up on water-rich foods like watermelon (92% water), cucumber (95%) and celery (95%).

BALANCE TIP#2
HYDRATION

It's no secret that water is the most vital resource for the human body, and yet most of us consume nowhere near the amount we need. Here are three ways you can stay hydrated and healthy in even the hottest summer.

- ### Spice it up:
  We know that always drinking plain water can be 'boring', so we recommend infusing it with fruit, spices and teas.

- ### Be environmentally friendly:
  Buy a reusable BPA-free drink bottle. It will act as a reminder to continually top up your water supply, and you'll also be cutting down on plastic consumption.

- ### Use technology:
  Set water reminders on your phone and use technology to improve your health.

'Don't eat anything your great grandmother wouldn't recognise as food'
—MICHAEL POLLAN

Gorgeous body-healing salads, superfood dressings, poke and lazy sushi, our balanced lunches are perfect to savour at home or to pack for school or work. These luscious wholefood recipes are super simple, save you time, and are nutritious and delicious.

SALADS 78

To make the perfect salad, it's all about getting the balance of textures and flavours spot on. Pick your favourite seasonal produce and ingredients, and mix and match them with a different dressing each time so you never get bored.

SUPERFOOD DRESSINGS 86

Way too many awesome, healing salads are ruined by dressings containing cheap preservatives and artificial ingredients. NEVER AGAIN! Say hello to our healthy superfood dressings — they're packed with flavour, good oils and just the right amount of acid to add zing to any of the above Bondi Harvest salads.

TARTINES 91

'Tartines' is basically a fancy word for yummy ingredients presented on top of a perfectly toasted piece of sourdough — or try our funky variation of a grilled slice of sweet potato instead! Avocado definitely leads the way for toppings, but don't deny your taste buds these other brilliant flavour combos.

POKE & LAZY SUSHI 94

Poke and sushi are two of the healthiest, simplest and tastiest ways to eat fresh seafood. Poke originated in Hawaii and traditionally is made with Ahi Tuna. The key to good poke — whether in a wrap, a crepe, rice paper roll or bowl — is super-fresh seafood paired with great textures for toppings. And our Lazy Sushi recipe is a sexy, satisfying way to make sushi at home, without the fuss or hassle.

WEEKEND LUNCHES 100

Weekends are the perfect time to slow it down and get creative in the kitchen, make a mess and try something different. Whether you're putting together a romantic picnic, BBQ with mates or a feast for one, our weekend lunches are designed to impress and inspire with bursting flavours and new cooking techniques.

GRAB & GO 112

Full-on healthy and fun energy balls, rice paper rolls and snacks designed to be enjoyed as quick bites at home or packed to take to work, the gym or the park. Basic everyday ingredients are treated with love to create mouthwatering and nutritious appetite-quenchers when you're on the go.

SALADS

TABASCO, KALE & COS LETTUCE SALAD

(V) *Serves 2—4*

1 bunch kale, trimmed
2 tablespoons olive oil
2 teaspoons Tabasco
finely grated zest and juice of 2 lemons
2 baby cos (romaine) lettuces, sliced
3 radishes, sliced
30 g (1 oz/¼ cup) currants
40 g (1½ oz/¼ cup) almonds, toasted
25 g (¾ oz/¼ cup) finely grated parmesan cheese
80 ml (2½ fl oz/⅓ cup) kombucha probiotic dressing (page 86)

Preheat the oven 180°C (350°F). Line 2 large baking trays with baking paper. Arrange the kale leaves on the trays in a single layer. Bake for 20 minutes, until wilted.

While the kale is still hot dress with olive oil, Tabasco, lemon zest and juice. Season with salt and pepper. Leave to cool.

Combine the kale with the lettuce, radishes, currants, almonds and parmesan. Toss with the kombucha probiotic dressing and serve.

CHICKPEA, KALE, RADISH RAINBOW SALAD

(GF) (V) (DF) (VE) *Serves 4*

720 g (24 oz/4 cups) cooked chickpeas
1 bunch kale, trimmed and chopped
2 carrots, coarsely grated or shredded into noodles
2 yellow zucchini (courgette), coarsely grated or shredded into noodles
4 radishes, finely sliced
1 cup mint leaves, chopped
1 teaspoon ground cumin
¼ cup pistachio dukkah (page 218)
finely grated zest of 3 lemons
5 tablespoons turmeric, citrus & ginger vinaigrette (page 87)
lemon wedges, to serve

Combine the chickpeas, kale, carrots, zucchini, radishes, mint, cumin, dukkah and lemon zest in a large bowl.

Dress with the vinaigrette, season with salt and pepper and toss to coat. Serve with lemon wedges.

HALF COS SALAD

(V) Serves 4

2 baby cos (romaine) lettuce, halved
2 tablespoons pepitas (pumpkin seeds)
2 hard-boiled eggs
3 radishes, finely sliced
4 lemon wedges

HAZELNUT BRIOCHE CRUMBS

130 g (4½ oz/1 cup) hazelnuts, finely chopped
1 tablespoon coriander seeds, toasted
1 tablespoon dried chilli flakes
2 tablespoons ground black pepper
1 tablespoon sea salt
finely grated zest of 1 lemon
300 ml (10½ fl oz) olive oil
3 cups coarse brioche crumbs
  (about 1 cm/½ inch pieces)

SALSA

1 avocado, diced
70 g (2½ oz/½ cup) cherry tomatoes,
  cut into quarters
¼ red onion, diced
½ garlic clove, minced
finely grated zest of 1 lemon
60 ml (2 fl oz/¼ cup) olive oil

To make the hazelnut brioche crumbs, preheat the oven to 180°C (350°F). Mix the hazelnuts, coriander seeds, chilli flakes, pepper, salt and lemon zest in a bowl. Add the olive oil and brioche crumbs and mix well. Scatter over a baking tray and bake, checking every 5 minutes, until golden brown and crunchy.

To make the salsa, mix all the ingredients together in a bowl and season with salt and pepper.

Arrange the lettuce halves on a platter or serving plates. Top with the salsa, some of the brioche crumbs (to taste) and the pepitas.

Finely grate the hard-boiled eggs over the lettuce, top with radish slices and serve with lemon wedges on the side.

NOTE: Remaining brioche crumb mix will keep for up to 2 weeks in an airtight container.

RAINBOW CARROT SALAD

(GF) (V) (DF) Serves 2

1 garlic clove, minced
2 cm (¾ inch) piece ginger, minced
5 thyme sprigs, leaves picked
1 pinch fennel seeds
½ teaspoon honey
finely grated zest and juice of 1 lime
1 bunch rainbow baby carrots, thinly sliced
1 fennel bulb, diced
1 nectarine, diced
80 g (2¾ oz/½ cup) almonds, chopped

Mix the garlic, ginger, thyme, fennel seeds, honey, lime zest and juice in a large bowl to make a dressing.

Add the carrots, fennel, nectarine and almonds. Toss with the dressing to coat.

Less fuss
MORE FLAVOUR

BROWN RICE SALAD

GF DF Serves 4–5

500 ml (17 fl oz/2 cups) chicken or vegetable stock
200 g (7 oz/1 cup) brown rice
1 cup mint leaves, finely chopped
1½ cups parsley leaves, finely chopped
½ red onion, diced
2 garlic cloves, minced
1 small red chilli, finely chopped
finely grated zest and juice of 2 lemons
4 tomatoes, deseeded and diced
80 ml (2½ fl oz/⅓ cup) olive oil
2 avocados, cut into quarters
2 grapefruits or oranges, segmented
½ cup kale, torn

Combine the stock and rice in a large pot and place over high heat. Bring to the boil, uncovered. As soon as it comes to the boil, cover with a lid and turn the heat down to low.

Simmer for 15–20 minutes, until the rice is tender and the stock has been absorbed.

Take off the stove and let sit for at least 10 minutes, then transfer to a container and cool.

Mix the brown rice, mint, parsley, onion, garlic, chilli, lemon zest, juice, tomato and olive oil, and arrange in a bowl with the avocado, citrus fruit and kale.

Season with salt and pepper and serve.

RAW SUMMER BEAN SALAD

GF V DF VE Serves 2–4

450 g (1 lb) green beans, trimmed
450 g (1 lb) sugar snap peas, trimmed
½ cup chopped silverbeet (Swiss chard) or purple kale
½ cup chimichurri (page 124)
225 g (8 oz) radishes, finely sliced
160 g (5½ oz/1 cup) almonds, toasted

Mix the beans, sugar snap peas, silverbeet and chimichurri together in a bowl.

Season with salt and pepper and transfer to a serving bowl.

Garnish with sliced radishes and almonds to serve.

SWEET & SOUR CARROT SALAD

GF **V** Serves 2–4

450 g (1 lb) baby carrots, trimmed and washed

2 tablespoons minced garlic

60 ml (2 fl oz/¼ cup) honey or maple syrup

60 ml (2 fl oz/¼ cup) olive oil

1 jalapeno chilli, minced

½ bunch thyme

2 teaspoons cumin seeds

1 teaspoon fennel seeds

60 ml (2 fl oz/¼ cup) white wine vinegar

2 bunches kale, trimmed, chopped

60 g (2 oz/½ cup) walnuts, toasted

50 g (1¾ oz/½ cup) finely grated parmesan cheese

Preheat the oven to 180°C (350°F).

Toss the carrots, garlic, honey, oil, jalapeno, thyme, cumin seeds and fennel seeds in a bowl until combined. Transfer to a large rimmed baking tray and bake for 20–30 minutes, until the carrots are tender.

While the mixture is still hot, drizzle with the vinegar and toss to deglaze the tray. Leave to cool.

To serve, mix the carrots with the kale, walnuts and parmesan.

RAW CHOPPED SUMMER SALAD

GF **V** **DF** **VE** Serves 2

1 Lebanese cucumber, diced

1 bunch mint, leaves picked

1 bunch dill, leaves picked

1 red capsicum (pepper), diced

1 green capsicum (pepper), diced

1 red onion, diced

180 g (6½ oz/1 cup) cooked black beans

1 cup chopped kale leaves

2 tablespoons turmeric, citrus & ginger vinaigrette (page 87)

Combine the cucumber, herbs, capsicums, onion, beans and kale in a large bowl.

Drizzle with the vinaigrette and toss to coat.

SUPERFOOD DRESSINGS

TAHINI CAESAR DRESSING

(GF) (DF) Makes 250 ml (8½ fl oz/1 cup)

135 g (4¾ oz/½ cup) homemade tahini (page 218)
finely grated zest and juice of 2-3 lemons (to taste)
1 garlic clove, minced
½ teaspoon cayenne pepper
½ teaspoon smoked paprika
2 anchovy fillets
¼ teaspoon capers
½ teaspoon sea salt

Combine all the ingredients with 60 ml (2 fl oz/¼ cup) water in a blender. Season with black pepper and blend until smooth. If you are after a runnier consistency, add a little more water.

This dressing will keep in an airtight container in the fridge for 2–3 weeks.

THAI DRESSING

(GF) (DF) Makes 250 ml (8½ fl oz/1 cup)

finely grated zest and juice of 3 limes
finely grated zest and juice of 1 lemon
2 tablespoons fish sauce
80 ml (2½ fl oz/⅓ cup) olive oil
1½ tablespoons palm sugar
2 teaspoons sesame oil
1 tablespoon finely grated fresh ginger
1 teaspoon sesame seeds, toasted

Mix all the ingredients together in a bowl or a jar. This dressing will keep in an airtight container in the fridge for 2–3 weeks.

KOMBUCHA PROBIOTIC VINAIGRETTE

(GF) (V) (DF) Makes 500 ml (17 fl oz/2 cups)

250 ml (9 fl oz/1 cup) kombucha (page 27)
250 ml (9 fl oz/1 cup) olive oil
2 tablespoons apple cider vinegar
1 teaspoon honey
1 tablespoon dried oregano
½ teaspoon thyme leaves
½ garlic clove, minced

Place everything into a blender, season with salt and pepper and blend until smooth. This dressing will keep in an airtight container in the fridge for 3–4 weeks.

MACADAMIA AIOLI

(GF) (V) (DF) (VE) Makes 500 ml (17 fl oz/2 cups)

140 g (5 oz/1 cup) raw macadamia nuts, soaked in water overnight
125 ml (4 fl oz/½ cup) almond milk
¼ teaspoon cayenne pepper
125 ml (4 fl oz/½ cup) extra virgin olive oil
1 tablespoon apple cider vinegar
finely grated zest and juice of 1 lemon
1 garlic clove, minced
½ teaspoon sea salt

Drain the macadamias and combine with the remaining ingredients in a food processor or a high-speed blender. Process to a smooth consistency.

Macadamia aioli will keep in an airtight container in the fridge for 2–3 weeks.

TURMERIC, CITRUS & GINGER VINAIGRETTE

(GF) (V) (DF) (VE) Makes 600 ml (20½ fl oz/2½ cups)

500 ml (17 fl oz/2 cups) olive oil
2 tablespoons apple cider vinegar
finely grated zest and juice of 1 lemon
finely grated zest and juice of 1 orange
finely grated zest and juice of 2 limes
½ teaspoon finely grated ginger
½ teaspoon ground turmeric
¼ teaspoon cayenne pepper

Place everything into a blender and blend until smooth. This dressing will keep in an airtight container in the fridge for 2–3 weeks.

CAYENNE FIRE BOMB

(GF) (V) (DF) (VE) Makes 1 litre (34 fl oz/4 cups)

750 ml (26 fl oz/3 cups) olive oil
125 ml (4 fl oz/½ cup) red wine vinegar
finely grated zest and juice of 2 lemons
1 teaspoon minced garlic
1 teaspoon finely grated fresh ginger
1 small red chilli, finely chopped
2 teaspoons cayenne pepper
½ teaspoon ground paprika
½ teaspoon freshly ground black pepper

Place all the ingredients into a food processor or blender. Use the pulse button to blend in short bursts, until smooth and combined.

This dressing will keep in an airtight container in the fridge for 3–4 weeks.

AVOCADO, LIME & CORIANDER

(GF) (V) Makes 750 ml (25½ fl oz/3 cups)

2 avocados, flesh scooped out
130 g (4 ½ oz/½ cup) Greek or homemade yoghurt (page 216)
125 ml (4 fl oz/½ cup) avocado or olive oil
finely grated zest and juice of 3 limes
⅓ cup coriander (cilantro) leaves, chopped
⅓ cup mint leaves, chopped
1 garlic clove, minced

Place all the ingredients into a food processor or blender. Use the pulse button to blend in short bursts, until smooth and combined. Don't over-blend it, as the heat will change the colour of the dressing.

If you are after a runnier consistency, add a little water.

This dressing will keep in an airtight container in the fridge for 3–4 days.

PONZU

(V) (DF) (VE) Makes 300 ml (10¼ fl oz/1⅓ cups)

125 ml (4 fl oz/½ cup) low-salt soy sauce
finely grated zest and juice of 2 lemons
finely grated zest and juice of 2 oranges
1½ tablespoons mirin (rice wine)
2 teaspoons ground black pepper
1 tablespoon finely chopped shallot
1 tablespoon sesame seeds, toasted

Mix all the ingredients together with 1 tablespoon water. Ponzu will keep in an airtight container in the fridge for 3–4 weeks.

TARTINES

Serves 4

These toppings are enough for 4 slices of toasted sourdough bread. Alternatively, for a gluten-free option, you can cut a sweet potato lengthways into 1 cm (½ inch) slices and toast in a toaster on medium heat, or under a grill (broiler), until tender and golden brown.

SWEET HALOUMI

(GF) (V)

1 tablespoon olive oil
8 slices haloumi
1 avocado, sliced
1 tablespoon honey
1 lemon, halved
1 tablespoon almonds, toasted and sliced

Heat the oil in a frying pan over medium-high heat. Cook the haloumi for 1–2 minutes each side or until golden.

Place haloumi on toast then top with avocado. Drizzle with honey and a squeeze of lemon. Sprinkle with almonds and season with sea salt and freshly ground black pepper.

SUMMER TOMATO, SEA SALT, FRIED EGG & BASIL

(GF) (V) (DF)

1 firm tomato
1 tablespoon chopped basil
1 teaspoon olive oil
1 teaspoon sea salt
1 teaspoon black pepper
4 eggs, fried

Grate the tomato into a bowl. Add the basil, olive oil, salt and pepper. Spoon mixture onto the toast then top with a fried egg.

BALSAMIC STRAWBERRIES & RICOTTA

(GF) (V)

60 ml (2 fl oz/¼ cup) balsamic vinegar
1 teaspoon honey
2 sprigs thyme
250 g (9 oz) strawberries, cleaned and kept whole
85 g (3 oz/¼ cup) ricotta
1 tablespoon hazelnuts, sliced

Combine balsamic, honey and thyme in a frying pan and cook over medium heat for 10 minutes or until reduced and syrupy. Add the strawberries. Cook for about 3 minutes, tossing to coat, until softened.

Spread toast with ricotta, then top with strawberries and hazelnuts.

RICOTTA & WILD PICKLED MUSHROOMS

(V)

2 tablespoons olive oil
1 garlic clove, chopped
1 sprig thyme, leaves picked
90 g (3 oz) mushrooms, cleaned and trimmed
1 cup chopped kale
1 teaspoon Tabasco
85 g (3 oz/¼ cup) ricotta
1 sprig parsley, leaves picked
1 tablespoon walnuts, toasted

Heat the oil in a frying pan over medium-high heat. Add the garlic, thyme and mushrooms and cook until tender. Add the kale and toss to wilt, then stir in the Tabasco and season with salt and pepper.

Spread ricotta onto the toast, and top with the mushroom mixture. Sprinkle with the parsley and toasted walnuts.

POKE & LAZY SUSHI

POKE BASE MIXTURE

DF *Serves 4–5*

250 g (9 oz) sustainable fish, diced
2 tablespoons soy sauce
2 tablespoons chopped coriander (cilantro) leaves
1 tablespoon sesame seeds
1 teaspoon sesame oil
2 cm (¾ inch) piece ginger, finely grated
1 garlic clove, minced
finely chopped red chilli, to taste
finely grated zest of 1 lemon

Mix the fish, soy sauce, coriander, sesame seeds, sesame oil, ginger, garlic, chilli and lemon zest in a glass or ceramic bowl.

Cover and marinate in the fridge for at least 30 minutes, but ideally overnight.

NOTE: Use fish such as dusky flathead, Australian salmon, whiting or Spanish mackerel. Replace the fish with tofu or mushrooms for a vegetarian version.

POKE BOWL

DF *Serves 4*

190 g (6¾ oz/1 cup) quinoa, cooked
1 quantity poke base mixture
2 tablespoons wakame seaweed
2 tablespoons wasabi peas
2 nori sheets, cut into fine strips

SALAD

85 g (3 oz/½ cup) edamame beans
1 avocado, halved and fanned
1 tablespoon chopped coriander (cilantro) leaves
2 spring onions (scallions), sliced
2 tablespoons kimchi (page 26)
2 tablespoons shredded white cabbage

Make a layer of quinoa in shallow bowls. Top with poke mixture, then the salad ingredients. Garnish with wakame seaweed, wasabi peas and some nori chips.

NOTE: Use brown rice instead of quinoa if you prefer.

POKE WRAP

DF Serves 4

1 cup watercress sprigs
½ cup coriander (cilantro) leaves
2 cm (¾ inch) piece ginger, julienned
1 quantity poke base mixture (page 94)
1 avocado, quartered

CREPES

130 g (4½ oz/1 cup) buckwheat flour
80 ml (2½ fl oz/⅓ cup) almond milk
1 egg, lightly beaten
1 tablespoon fish sauce
1 tablespoon sesame seeds
1 teaspoon sesame oil
½ teaspoon chilli paste
2 nori sheets, crumbled
coconut oil, for cooking

To make the crepes, combine the buckwheat flour, milk, egg, fish sauce, sesame seeds, sesame oil, chilli paste and nori in a mixing bowl. Mix until smooth and evenly combined.

Heat a little coconut oil in a small frying pan over medium heat. Pour enough mixture into the pan to cover in a thin layer and then cook on each side for approximately 1 minute. Repeat with remaining batter to make 4 crepes.

Mix the watercress, coriander and ginger together. Divide the poke mixture between the crepes, top with the greens and ginger and the avocado. Roll up to enclose.

LAZY SUSHI

DF Serves 4

190 g (6¾ oz/1 cup) quinoa, cooked
85 g (3 oz/½ cup) edamame beans
2 spring onions (scallions), sliced
1 avocado, sliced
1 tablespoon chopped coriander (cilantro) leaves
ponzu (page 87), to taste
250 g (9 oz) sashimi-grade salmon, diced
3 nori sheets, cut into pieces
sesame salt (page 219), to taste

In a bowl, mix the quinoa, edamame, spring onions, avocado, coriander and ponzu to taste.

Divide mixture between bowls or plates.

Top with diced salmon, nori sheets and sesame salt. Serve extra ponzu on the side.

NOTE: Replace the quinoa with brown rice, if you prefer.

Marinated in probiotic yoghurt and anti-inflammatory spices, my Tandoori salmon and homemade flatbread is an action-packed, aromatic flavour bomb. And if that's not enough, it's also quick and simple to prepare.

TANDOORI SALMON SKEWERS WITH TURMERIC FLATBREAD

Serves 4

520 g (1 lb 2½ oz/2 cups) Greek or homemade yoghurt (page 216)

finely grated zest and juice of 1 lemon

2 teaspoons ground turmeric

1 teaspoon ground cinnamon

1 teaspoon ground cumin

1 teaspoon ground allspice

2 teaspoons ground paprika

1 teaspoon cayenne pepper

1 teaspoon ground black pepper

1 garlic clove, minced

1 teaspoon finely grated fresh ginger

500 g (1 lb 2 oz) fresh salmon, cut into 3 cm (1¼ inch) cubes

4 turmeric flatbreads (page 214)

3 cups chickpea, kale, radish rainbow salad (page 79)

YOGHURT SAUCE

1 Lebanese cucumber, sliced

260 g (9¼ oz/1 cup) Greek or homemade yoghurt (page 216)

2 tablespoons chopped mint

finely grated zest and juice of 1 lime

Combine the yoghurt, lemon zest, juice, turmeric, cinnamon, cumin, allspice, paprika, cayenne pepper, black pepper, garlic, ginger and a pinch of sea salt in a glass or ceramic mixing bowl. Mix to a smooth paste. Add the salmon and gently massage to coat in the marinade. Cover and let marinate for 12–24 hours in the fridge.

If you are using wooden skewers soak them in water for about an hour first to stop them burning during cooking (you'll need 10). Thread the fish onto skewers.

Heat a large frying pan or BBQ over medium-high heat. Cook the salmon for about 1–2 minutes on each side, until cooked but still tender in the middle.

To make the yoghurt sauce, mix the cucumber, yoghurt, mint, lime zest and juice in a bowl and season well with salt and pepper.

To serve, smear a tablespoon of yoghurt sauce in the middle of a flatbread, then top with salmon and the chickpea salad.

These falafels are baked — not deep-fried — making them lower in bad fats, safer to cook and much easier to clean up after when you're finished. Served with my super-zesty tabbouleh and yoghurt dressing, it's perfectly balanced to tingle your tastebuds.

BAKED QUINOA FALAFEL ON BROWN RICE TABOULI WITH YOGHURT DRESSING

(V) *Serves 4—6*

FALAFEL

180 g (6 oz/1 cup) cooked chickpeas

60 g (2 oz/½ cup) cooked quinoa

25 g (¾ oz/¼ cup) almond meal

2 garlic cloves

¼ red onion, finely chopped

finely grated zest of 1 lemon

¼ cup flat-leaf parsley leaves

⅓ cup coriander (cilantro) leaves

½ teaspoon ground cumin

½ teaspoon ground coriander

¼ teaspoon cayenne pepper

½ teaspoon baking powder

1 egg, lightly beaten

2-3 tablespoons coconut oil

2 tablespoons olive oil

BROWN RICE TABOULI

200 g (7 oz/1 cup) brown rice, cooked and cooled

1½ cups parsley leaves, chopped

1 cup mint leaves, chopped

½ red onion, finely chopped

2 garlic cloves, minced

1 small red chilli, finely chopped

finely grated zest and juice of 1 lemon

4 tomatoes, deseeded and diced

60 ml (2 fl oz/¼ cup) olive oil

2 tablespoons grated horseradish

BEETROOT HUMMUS

½ cup hummus (page 218)

3 tablespoons grated beetroot (beet)

YOGHURT DRESSING

260 g (9¼ oz/1 cup) Greek or homemade yoghurt (page 216)

finely grated zest and juice of 2 lemons

To make the falafels, preheat the oven to 200°C (400°F) and line a baking tray with baking paper.

Combine all the ingredients (except the olive oil) in a food processor and pulse until everything comes together. Spoon out desired sized falafel balls onto a plate lined with baking paper, then place the plate in the fridge for 15 minutes to firm up.

Heat the olive oil in a frying pan over medium heat. Cook falafels in batches for 3 minutes on each side, until golden brown. Transfer to the baking tray and bake for 15 minutes to warm through.

To make the brown rice tabouli, mix everything together and season with salt and pepper.

To make the beetroot hummus, mix hummus and grated beetroot in a bowl. Make the yoghurt dressing by mixing the yoghurt, lemon zest and juice in a bowl.

Spoon beetroot hummus onto serving plates and scatter with brown rice tabbouli. Top with falafels and yoghurt dressing.

Caramelising pumpkin always adds a new level of flavour and complexity to this simple ingredient, making it ideal for your next BBQ. Sliced fine and cooked on a hot grill, serve it flat and topped with a fresh, acidic seasonal salad. It's guaranteed to impress.

WEEKEND LUNCHES WEEKEND

BBQ PUMPKIN CARPACCIO SALAD

GF V *Serves 4–5*

1 butternut pumpkin
2 tablespoons olive oil
2 lemons, cut into segments
2 oranges, cut into segments
1 cup mint leaves
4 radishes, thinly sliced
3 tablespoons almonds chopped
120 g (4 oz/1 cup) pepitas (pumpkin seeds)
260 g (9¼ oz/1 cup) ricotta, crumbled (optional)

Halve the pumpkin lengthways, then cut crossways into 1 cm (½ inch) slices.

Preheat a BBQ over medium-high heat. Toss pumpkin slices with oil and season with salt and pepper.

Cook on the BBQ for about 5 minutes each side, until tender and coloured.

Combine the citrus segments, mint leaves and radishes in a bowl.

Lay pumpkin flat on a platter then top with the citrus salad. Scatter with pepitas, almonds and ricotta (if using).

Hearty and packed with protein, my vegetarian beetroot and lentil burger is a healthy wholefood feast all wrapped up in a bun for easy two-handed eating. Even the vegetarian sceptics will be coming back for more of this little beauty!

BEETROOT LENTIL BURGER

Ⓥ Serves 6

2 teaspoons olive oil

1 onion, finely chopped

2 garlic cloves, minced

1 small red chilli, finely chopped

250 g (9 oz) cooked brown lentils

325 g (11 oz) raw beetroot (beet), grated

1 egg

1 teaspoon ground turmeric

1 teaspoon garam masala

2 teaspoons smoked paprika

1 teaspoon finely grated fresh ginger

6 tablespoons plain (all-purpose) flour, cornmeal or almond meal

1 tablespoon olive oil, extra

6 slices peeled fresh pineapple

160 g (5½ oz/2 cups) shredded cabbage

2 tomatoes, sliced

260 g (9 oz/1 cup) natural or homemade yoghurt (page 216)

6 brioche, sourdough or gluten-free buns

turmeric crispy chickpeas (page 116), to serve (optional)

Heat the olive oil in a frying pan over medium heat. Cook the onion, garlic and chilli until soft. Transfer to a plate and place into the fridge to cool.

In a large bowl, mix the lentils, cooled onion mixture, beetroot, egg, turmeric, garam masala, paprika and ginger until combined. Season with salt and pepper, then sprinkle in the flour (or cornmeal or almond meal) one tablespoon at a time, until the mixture is dry and firm enough to hold together.

Shape mixture into 6 individual patties. Place onto a tray and chill in the fridge for 10 minutes to firm up.

Heat the extra olive oil in a large non-stick frying pan over medium heat. Add the lentil patties and cook for 5–6 minutes each side, until caramelised and heated through.

Lay out all the remaining ingredients on a large chopping board with the warm patties and let people construct their own burgers. Season with salt and pepper. Serve with the turmeric chickpeas (if using) on the side.

TIP: Make the patties ahead of time and freeze them for speed and convenience.

I love to serve tender and flavour-packed octopus every time with a fresh sweet, salty and sour salad made with haloumi, currants and pomegranate. A great recipe to bring out while entertaining — fancy yet foolproof.

SWEET & SALTY OCTOPUS SALAD

GF Serves 4–5

1 teapoon sea salt

1 tablespoon fennel seeds

1 bay leaf

1 sprig rosemary

1 sprig thyme

1 lemon, sliced

400 g (14 oz) octopus tentacles, tenderised

65 g (2 oz/⅓ cup) toasted buckwheat

40 g (1½ oz/⅓ cup) cooked quinoa

1 tablespoon currants

1 tablespoon finely diced fennel

2 radishes, finely sliced

¼ cup mint leaves

1 teaspoon pomegranate seeds

4 tablespoons olive oil

finely grated zest and juice 1 lemon

200 g (7 oz) haloumi, diced

To cook the octopus, place 2 litres (2 quarts/8 cups) water in a large saucepan. Add salt, fennel seeds, bay leaf, rosemary, thyme and lemon. Bring to the boil then simmer for 5 minutes.

Add the octopus and simmer for 40–50 minutes, until tender. Remove from pan and set aside to rest.

In a mixing bowl, combine the buckwheat, quinoa, currants, fennel, radishes, mint, pomegranate, 3 tablespoons olive oil, lemon zest and juice.

Heat the remaining oil in a frying pan over medium heat. Cook haloumi for 2–3 minutes, stirring and turning occasionally, until golden brown. While still warm add to the salad and toss well.

Arrange the salad on a large board and top with the octopus tentacles.

NOTE: To tenderise the octopus, beat with a meat mallet or rolling pin for 15 minutes.

Peanut Oat Bombs, Green Power, Immune Booster or Double Dark Chocolate: choose your energy weapon for midday (or all-day) snacking. Take these to work or have them sitting around the house to give you that little guilt-free, long-lasting energy hit when you need it most.

ENERGY BALLS

PEANUT OAT BOMBS

(V) (DF) Makes 20

90 g (3 oz/1 cup) rolled oats
140 g (5 oz/½ cup) peanut butter
½ cup antioxidant immune boost protein powder (page 22)
60 g (2 oz/½ cup) cocoa nibs
80 ml (2½ fl oz/⅓ cup) honey
1 tablespoon chia seeds
1 teaspoon vanilla extract

GREEN POWER

(GF) (V) (DF) Makes 12

4 Medjool dates, pitted, soaked in boiling water for 5 minutes, then drained and puréed until smooth
1 cup super green protein powder (page 23)
1 tablespoon honey
1 tablespoon chia seeds
2 teaspoons finely chopped mint leaves
finely grated zest of 1 lemon

DOUBLE DARK CHOCOLATE

(V) Makes 16

1 cup chocolate protein powder (page 23)
60 g (2 oz/½ cup) cocoa nibs
35 g (1¼ oz/⅓ cup) almond meal
60 ml (2 oz/¼ cup) honey
1 tablespoon chia seeds
1 teaspoon activated charcoal

IMMUNE BOOSTER

(GF) (V) (DF) Makes 24

1 cup antioxidant immune boost protein powder (page 22)
50 g (1¾ oz/½ cup) almond meal
35 g (1¼ oz/½ cup) shredded coconut
55 g (1¾ oz/⅓ cup) chia seeds
80 ml (2½ fl oz/⅓ cup) honey
5 tablespoons coconut water

The following method works for all four energy ball flavours.

Mix all the ingredients together until evenly combined. Place in the fridge until firm. Roll tablespoons of mixture into balls.

Store in an airtight container in the fridge for up to 2 weeks.

*Rice paper rolls are a great lean, gluten-free substitute for sandwiches.
Think outside the box and fill them with your favourite combinations:
dinner leftovers, fruit salad or desserts — you name it!
It's all good. Wrap them, pack them and take them to work or the beach.*

RICE PAPER ROLLS

RAINBOW WRAP

(V) (VE)

4 rice paper sheets (22cm/8½ inch)
150 g (5½ oz/1 cup) raw cauliflower rice
1 cup salt fermented vegetables (page 26), chopped
1 avocado, cut in quarters
1 carrot, grated
½ cup basil leaves

CHICKEN

(DF)

4 rice paper sheets (22cm/8½ inch)
½ cup shredded chicken (miso mushroom roasted
  chicken, page 152)
1 tablespoon macadamia aioli (page 86)
2 mango cheeks, sliced
1 cup rocket (arugula)
1 tablespoon shredded coconut, toasted

FRUIT SALAD

(GF) (V)

4 rice paper sheets (22cm/8½ inch)
2 kiwi fruits, sliced
3 strawberries, sliced
1 banana, sliced
½ cup chia seed pudding of your choice (pages 42-43)
½ cup mint leaves

CHOCOLATE BROWN RICE PUDDING

(GF) (V)

4 rice paper sheets (22cm/8½ inch)
1 cup healthy black forest brown rice breakfast pudding
  (page 39)
1 banana, sliced
3 strawberries, sliced

SALMON SUSHI

(GF) (DF)

4 rice paper sheets (22cm/8½ inch)
4 nori seaweed sheets
200 g (7 oz) sashimi-grade salmon, sliced
1 avocado, cut in quarters
½ cup coriander (cilantro) leaves
120 g (4 oz/1 cup) cooked quinoa

POKE RICE PAPER ROLLS

(DF)

4 rice paper sheets (22 cm/8½ inch)
120 g (4 oz/1 cup) cooked quinoa
1 quantity poke base mixture (page 94)
1 avocado, cut into quarters
½ cup coriander (cilantro) leaves
½ cup mint leaves
85 g (3 oz/½ cup) edamame beans

Place some warm water into a shallow dish large enough
to hold a sheet of rice paper. Lay out a clean tea towel.

Working one at a time, place a sheet of rice paper into
the water and leave for about 15 seconds, until soft and
translucent. Transfer it to the clean tea towel, fold the
towel over and dab the rice paper dry. Open the tea
towel.

Place ¼ of the filling into the middle of the rice paper.
Fold the sides over and roll up firmly to enclose. Repeat
with remaining rice paper and filling.

Store in an airtight container in the fridge, with baking
paper between each roll to stop them from sticking
together. They will last up to 3 days.

NOTE: You can use green tea in place of the water for
soaking, if you like.

SNACKS

NORI SEAWEED CHIPS

V DF VE Makes 8 chips

7 nori sheets
2 cups ponzu (page 87)
1 tablespoon sesame seeds
1 teaspoon cayenne pepper
sea salt, to taste

Preheat the oven to 135°C (275°F) and line a baking tray with baking paper.

Lay one sheet of nori on the baking tray then, using a pastry brush, lightly brush with ponzu, making sure you reach the edges.

Place another nori sheet on top and repeat this process 6 times then, using scissors, cut nori stack into desired shapes and sprinkle with sea salt.

Bake for 15 minutes until crispy. Store in an airtight container.

TURMERIC CRISPY CHICKPEAS

GF V DF VE Makes 1 cup

180 g (6 oz/1 cup) cooked chickpeas
1 teaspoon ground turmeric
⅓ teaspoon ground cumin
finely grated zest of 1 lemon
¼ teaspoon cayenne pepper
⅓ teaspoon garlic powder

Preheat the oven to 170°C (340°F) and line a baking tray with baking paper.

Using paper towel, dry the chickpeas thoroughly. Place into a bowl with the remaining ingredients and mix well.

Transfer to the prepared tray and roast for 1 hour or until crisp. Cool completely.

Store in an airtight container, at room temperature, for up to 2 days.

QUINOA BITES

GF V DF Makes 10

100 g (3½ oz/1 cup) quinoa flakes
1 tablespoon metabolism booster protein powder (page 22)
1 tablespoon shredded coconut
1 tablespoon goji berries
1 banana, mashed
1 teaspoon honey

Preheat the oven to 180°C (350°F) and line a baking tray with baking paper.

Mix everything together, then spoon out onto the baking tray, leaving a little space in between for spreading. Bake for 15-20 minutes, until golden brown and firm.

Store in an airtight container in a dry place for up to 1 week.

STUFFED DATES

V DF VE Makes 10

50 g (1¾ oz/½ cup) almond meal
2 tablespoons coconut flakes
1 tablespoon 100% raw cacao powder
1 tablespoon protein powder
1 tablespoon spirulina
1 tablespoon chia seeds
100 ml (3½ fl oz) coconut water
10 Medjool dates

Combine the almond meal, coconut flakes, cacao, protein powder, spirulina, chia seeds and coconut water in a bowl. Mix well until combined.

Slit the dates lengthways and remove the seeds, without splitting dates in half. Stuff the dates with the almond mixture, and press the opening together to enclose filling.

Store in an airtight container in the fridge for up to 2 weeks.

BALANCE TIP#3
TECH DETOX

Now more than ever, we are connected to and reliant on technology. Smart phones, computers and apps have become an extension of us and are a part of our everyday lives.

This overload of information and connectivity comes with many positives, but there are also negative influences — and this is where our Bondi Harvest Technology Detox comes into play.

It is super simple and doesn't require you to download any app or spend any extra money. Instead, it's a series of small hints, tricks and changes that you can make to give your body and mind a break from both phone radiation and stimulation.

First things first: remove all electronic gadgets from the bedroom. Your bedroom is a place of rest. Phones, tablets, TVs and laptops are all impacting your sleep in ways you may not even notice.

- **Blue light woes:**
  The blue light from our devices impacts on the body's production of melatonin, the hormone that controls our sleep cycle. To help get your sleep cycle back on track, avoid using electronics at least half an hour before bed; pick up a book instead.

- **Be kind, unwind:**
  Emails, social media and screen entertainment all stimulate brain activity and can often trick our brain into thinking we need to stay awake. If you want your mind to unwind before bed, leave the phone alone.

- **Do not disturb:**
  Even as we sleep the vibrations, lights and sounds from notifications on our phones are still stimulating our brains and affecting our ability to stay asleep. So when it's time for bed, set your phone to 'do not disturb'.

- **Charge it elsewhere:**
  Plug your phone in away from your bed, preferably in another room entirely.

- **Get an alarm clock:**
  If you wake up to a phone alarm, you'll be more tempted to start checking emails and social media the minute your eyes are open.

- **Turn off app notifications:**
  Turning off those sound and screen notifications will lessen the temptation to check your phone unnecessarily.

- **No devices with meals:**
  Ban phones at the dinner table, whether you're out to dinner or at home.

- **Turn off 3G and 4G:**
  When you're out and about, at dinner or having coffee with a friend, you'll be less likely to play with apps on your phone if 3G and 4G aren't enabled.

- **Leave your phone at home:**
  Commit to one activity a day where you don't have your phone with you.

DINNER

'When we try to pick out anything by itself from nature we find it hitched to everything else in the universe.' — JOHN MUIR

Bondi Harvest dinners are all about falling in love with the humblest of ingredients, saving time and finishing the day stress-free with the perfect meal. We'll teach you how simple and easy it is to prepare delicious and healthy food, and how to turn everyday ingredients into feasts fit for a king, queen and your family.

NOT SO PASTA PASTA & PASTA SAUCES 124

I'm a chef and I adore and respect everything about pasta: the taste, the history and especially the nonnas! I'd never pretend that Zoodles, or courgetti, are actual pasta. BUT veggie pasta are so much fun to make, they're cheap and delicious, and are great substitutes if you want to lower your carb intake. (They're also a cool way to secretly pack veggies into meals for kids who aren't quite yet on the vegetable-loving bandwagon!)

And whether you're using Vegetti (vegetable 'spaghetti') or real pasta, our simple and nutrition-packed pasta sauces are the perfect complement for whichever option you go with.

THE HUMBLE CAULIFLOWER 132

I'll drop the L-bomb and tell everyone my dirty little secret: I'm in LOVE with the cauliflower! Roasted whole, in soups, as a pizza base, as rice or risotto and now a steak! The list goes on ... Wait till you see just how damn versatile and amazing the modest cauliflower really is.

VEGETARIAN DINNERS 144

Vegetarian cooking is all about respect — understanding the freshest and most commonplace seasonal produce and using good technique and imagination to really make your meals sing with flavour. These awesome recipes will make even the most committed carnivore weak at the knees!

ONE-POT WONDERS 152

The ultimate way to save time in the kitchen is to pack your ingredients into one pot and let time do the talking. Slow-cooked soups and stocks — no explanation needed, you know it's going to be good! Pop it into the oven or in your slow-cooker in the morning, and return to a delicious-smelling home and a delicious-tasting meal! (Just make doubly sure the oven temperature is nice and low before you leave the house.)

WEEKEND DINNERS 158

Spend a little extra time on the weekends to create these scrumptious and impressive dishes to share with your family, mates and/or partner — or to just give yourself a special treat. Go on, you know you want to, hahaha!

NOT SO PASTA PASTA

Vegetable pasta is such a great way to get extra veggies into your diet. It is simple to make, versatile and super cheap. Get creative and mix up veggies for different colours, flavours and textures – the options are endless! Here are my top three to get you started.

MANDOLIN

Use a mandolin to slice your vegetable into thin, wide ribbons. Then, with a sharp knife, slice these ribbons into long matchsticks or spaghetti-shaped strips.

VEGETTI/SPIRALISER

Wash and peel your favourite vegetable, and then slice the end so it fits into your Vegetti or spiraliser. Then simply follow the instructions on the machine. Definitely the quickest and simplest way to make vegetable spaghetti.

KNIFE SKILLS (OLD SCHOOL)

Personally, I like rocking it old school with a sharp knife and a solid chopping board. Simply trim the rounded sides of each vegetable to create a square or rectangle shape. Cut each piece lengthwise to create thin, wide ribbons. Then using a sharp knife, slice these ribbons into long matchsticks or spaghetti-shaped strips.

NOTE: Store a large batch in water in an airtight container in the fridge for up to 5 days.

PASTA SAUCES

CHIMICHURRI

(GF) (V) (DF) (VE) *Makes 2 cups*

1 firmly packed cup chopped parsley leaves
1 firmly packed cup chopped coriander (cilantro) leaves
½ firmly packed cup chopped oregano leaves
1 garlic clove, chopped
250 ml (9 fl oz/1 cup) extra virgin olive oil
1½ tablespoons red wine vinegar
1 tablespoon balsamic vinegar
finely grated zest of 1 lemon
small pinch dried chilli flakes

To make a rustic chimichurri, combine all the ingredients in a bowl. Season with salt and pepper and mix well.

For a smooth chimichurri, combine all the ingredients in a food processor or blender. Season with salt and pepper and blend until smooth.

Store chimichurri in an airtight container in the fridge for up to a week.

PASSATA

(GF) (V) (DF) (VE) Makes 500 ml (17 fl oz)

80 ml (2½ fl oz/⅓ cup) olive oil
1 white onion, diced
6 garlic cloves, minced
1 teaspoon finely chopped red chilli
500 ml (17 fl oz/2 cups) red wine
4 x 400 g (14 oz) cans diced tomatoes
1 teaspoon brown sugar
⅓ cup basil leaves, chopped
⅓ cup sage leaves, chopped
⅓ cup oregano leaves, chopped

Heat the olive oil in a large saucepan over medium heat. Add the onion, garlic and chilli, and cook until soft but not coloured. Add the red wine and simmer until reduced by two-thirds.

Add the tomatoes, sugar, basil, sage and oregano. Cook for 30 minutes until thick and dark in colour, stirring every few minutes to stop it sticking to the bottom.

Season with salt and pepper to taste. Serve over pasta or store in an airtight container in the fridge for 2–3 weeks.

MUSHROOM RAGU

(GF) (V) Serves 4

80 ml (2 ½ fl oz/⅓ cup) olive oil
2 garlic cloves, minced
1 small red chilli, finely chopped
½ fennel bulb, diced
1 small leek, sliced
135 g (4¾ oz/1½ cups) mixed mushrooms
100 g (3½ oz) butter, chopped (or 100 ml/3½ fl oz olive oil)
½ bunch parsley, leaves picked
½ bunch sage, leaves picked
finely grated zest and juice of 1 lemon
60 g (2 oz/½ cup) walnuts

Heat the olive oil in a frying pan over medium heat. Add the garlic, chilli, fennel and leek. Cook for a few minutes, until tender but not coloured. Add the mushrooms and cook until tender and slightly caramelised.

Finish the ragu by adding butter, parsley, sage, lemon zest, juice and walnuts. Season with salt and pepper to taste. Serve with your favourite pasta.

PESTO

(GF) (V) Makes 400 ml (13½ fl oz)

3 garlic cloves, minced
100 g (3½ oz) pine nuts, toasted
2 packed cups basil leaves
½ cup chopped kale
50 g (1¾ oz/½ cup) finely grated parmesan cheese
200 ml (7 fl oz) extra virgin olive oil
1 tablespoon walnuts
1 small handful microherbs

Combine the garlic, pine nuts, basil, kale and parmesan in a food processor (or use a mortar and pestle). Process or bash until roughly chopped. Slowly add the oil, processing continually to the desired consistency. Season with salt and pepper to taste.

Serve with your favourite pasta, and garnish with walnuts and microherbs.

VARIATIONS

Tomato (rosso) pesto
Add 200 g (7 oz) sundried tomatoes

Beetroot pesto
Add 70 g (2½ oz) chopped roasted beetroot

Pistachio
Swap pine nuts for 150 g (5½ oz) toasted pistachios

Avocado
Add flesh of ½ avocado, ⅓ cup coriander (cilantro) leaves and 1 minced small red chilli

GREEN SALSA

(GF) (DF) Makes 2 cups

250 ml (9 fl oz/1 cup) olive oil
⅓ cup mint leaves, chopped
⅓ cup parsley leaves, chopped
⅓ cup oregano leaves, chopped
1 teaspoon capers, finely chopped
1 teaspoon finely chopped anchovy
1 garlic clove, minced
finely grated zest and juice of 1 lemon

Mix all the ingredients in a bowl and season with salt and pepper.

Store in an airtight container in the fridge for 2 weeks.

VEGETARIAN BOLOGNESE

(GF) (V) (DF) (VE) Makes 1 litre (34 fl oz)

1 eggplant, diced
80 ml (2½ fl oz/⅓ cup) olive oil
1 onion, diced
1 carrot, diced
1 celery stalk, diced
1 red capsicum (pepper), diced
3 garlic cloves, minced
1 small red chilli, finely chopped
¼ teaspoon cayenne pepper
135 g (4¾ oz/1½ cups) mixed mushrooms,
  cleaned and quartered
1 tablespoon tomato paste (concentrated purée)
750 ml (26 fl oz/3 cups) red wine
750 ml (26 fl oz/3 cups) tomato purée
1 bunch oregano, leaves picked
1 bunch sage, leaves picked

Preheat the oven to 180°C (350°F). Arrange the eggplant onto a baking tray and bake for 10 minutes, until golden and soft.

Heat the oil in a saucepan over medium heat. Add the onion, carrot, celery, capsicum, garlic, chilli and cayenne pepper. Cook until tender and slightly coloured. Add the mushrooms and cook until tender, then stir in the tomato paste.

Pour in the red wine and stir to deglaze. Bring to a simmer and cook for 25–30 minutes, until reduced by two-thirds.

Add the eggplant, tomato purée, oregano and sage. Cook for a further 20–30 minutes, until the bolognese is thick and rich in colour and flavour. Season with salt and pepper.

PEPPERONATA

(GF) (V) (DF) (VE) Serves 4

80 ml (2½ fl oz/⅓ cup) olive oil
4 garlic cloves, minced
1 small red chilli, finely chopped
1 red onion, sliced
3 yellow capsicums (peppers), sliced
3 red capsicums (peppers), sliced
1 teaspoon brown sugar
50 g (1¾ oz/⅓ cup) almonds, toasted and chopped
50 g (1¾ oz/⅓ cup) pitted kalamata olives, sliced
⅓ cup sage leaves, chopped
⅓ cup parsley leaves, chopped
60 ml (2 fl oz/¼ cup) red wine vinegar

Heat the olive oil in a frying pan on medium heat. Add the garlic, chilli, onion and capsicum and cook for about 4 minutes or until tender.

Add the sugar, almonds, olives and herbs. Cook for a further 3–4 minutes, until the vegetables have caramelised sightly. Deglaze with red wine vinegar and season with salt and pepper.

Serve with your favourite pasta, or as a side dish.

Whole roasted vegetables are super simple to cook, and with a few tricks up your sleeve you can create incredibly tasty and healthy dishes with ease. Roast your cauliflower crusted with spices on a bed of orange, and this humble vegetable becomes crunchy on the outside yet steamed with orange juice in the centre. OMG.

BAKED TURMERIC CAULIFLOWER

GF V *Serves 3—5*

1 teaspoon ground turmeric

2 garlic cloves, minced

1 cm (½ inch) piece ginger, finely grated

½ teaspoon dried chilli flakes

1 orange, zest finely grated, sliced

160 ml (5½ fl oz/⅔ cup) coconut or olive oil

1 whole cauliflower, leaves trimmed

1 cup mint leaves

1 cup parsley leaves

140 g (5 oz/1 cup) cherry or baby heirloom tomatoes, halved

1 red onion, finely sliced

1 tablespoon sultanas (golden raisins) or currants

1 tablespoon apple cider vinegar

1 teaspoon smoked paprika

130 g (4½ oz/½ cup) Greek or homemade yoghurt (page 216)

1 tablespoon slivered almonds, toasted

Preheat the oven to 180°C (350°F).

Combine the turmeric, garlic, ginger, chilli, lemon zest and oil to make a paste.

Lay the orange slices into a roasting pan and place the cauliflower on top. Pour and spoon the spice paste over the top of the cauliflower, ensuring it's completely covered.

Cover with foil and bake for 1 hour 15 minutes or until tender. Remove the foil and bake for a further 25 minutes, until golden brown.

Mix the mint, parsley, tomatoes, onion, sultanas, vinegar and paprika until well combined.

Serve the roasted cauliflower on a bed of the tomato salad, then garnish with yoghurt and toasted almonds.

The more I cook and experiment with cauliflower the more I fall in love with it. This white, brainy-looking flavour sponge just keeps on delivering the goods. Cut your cauliflower into a cross-section, then grill it like you would a regular steak. The flavour and texture are divine.

CAULIFLOWER STEAK WITH BEETROOT HUMMUS

GF V DF *Serves 2–3*

1 small cauliflower
2 tablespoons olive oil
1 bunch thyme
1 lemon, sliced
1 cup rainbow carrot salad (page 80)

BEETROOT HUMMUS

360 g (12½ oz/2 cups) cooked chickpeas
150 g (5½ oz/1 cup) grated beetroot
2 tablespoons olive oil
2 tablespoons homemade tahini (page 218)
1 garlic clove
finely grated zest and juice of 1 lemon

Preheat the oven to 180°C (350°F). Line a large baking tray with baking paper.

Cut the cauliflower in half or thirds and then trim the outside sections to create 2 or 3 thick steaks.

Heat the oil in a large frying pan over medium heat. Cook the cauliflower for about 10 minutes each side, until caramelised.

Transfer the cauliflower to the baking tray. Season with salt and pepper and top with thyme and lemon slices. Bake for 15–20 minutes, until soft and golden.

To make the beetroot hummus, place the chickpeas, beetroot, olive oil, tahini, garlic, lemon zest and juice into a blender or food processor and blend until combined and smooth. Season with salt and pepper to taste.

Remove the thyme and lemon. Serve cauliflower steaks with beetroot hummus and rainbow carrot salad.

Is it a Risotto? Well, not really — it's raw, and there's no rice involved.

But when you cut your cauliflower up like this, you get riced cauliflower! Mix it with a delicious wet guacamole and you have a super-tasty raw, vegan 'risotto'.

RAW CAULIFLOWER RISOTTO

GF V DF VE *Serves 2—3*

1 avocado
finely grated zest and juice of 1 lemon
2 tablespoons olive oil
150 g (5½ oz/1 cup) raw cauliflower rice
1 cup chopped mint leaves
1 cup chopped coriander (cilantro) leaves
1 garlic clove, minced
3 tablespoons toasted slivered almonds
1 small handful of snow pea sprouts

Combine the avocado flesh, lemon zest, juice and olive oil in a bowl and season with salt and pepper. Mix to a smooth paste.

Add the cauliflower, herbs and garlic, and mix to combine. Serve sprinkled with the almonds and snow pea sprouts.

two serves please

Crispy, light and golden — without any of the post-pizza guilt. You can now have pizza every day of the week, ha ha ha! Our gluten-free cauliflower pizza base is packed with protein, it's simple to make, and you can adjust the spices and flavouring of the base to your liking. Gone are the days when pizza topping trumped the pizza base itself!

CAULIFLOWER PIZZA BASE

GF **V** *Serves 4—5*

600 g (1 lb 5 ½ oz/4 cups) raw cauliflower rice
1 egg, lightly beaten
50 g (1¾ oz/½ cup) almond meal
35 g (1¼ oz/⅓ cup) grated parmesan cheese
1 teaspoon cayenne pepper
finely grated zest of 1 lemon
1 teaspoon dried oregano
pinch of salt

Preheat the oven to 200°C (400°F). Line a baking tray with baking paper.

Bring a large saucepan of water to the boil. Add the cauliflower rice, cover and cook for 4-5 minutes. Drain well. When cool enough to handle, transfer to a clean tea towel. Gather the ends to enclose, and twist firmly to squeeze out all the remaining liquid.

Combine the cauliflower rice, egg, almond meal, parmesan, cayenne pepper, lemon zest, oregano and salt. Mix well until evenly combined.

Press the 'dough' out onto the baking tray, making sure it is evenly about 5 mm (¼ inch) thick. Bake for 35-40 minutes, until firm and golden.

Add toppings (see page 140 for suggestions), then return the pizza to oven for 5-10 minutes. Serve hot.

THE
Humble
CAULIFLOWER

PIZZA TOPPINGS

PESTO SALAD PIZZA

GF V

¼ cup pesto (page 126)

2 bulbs buffalo mozzarella, pulled apart into 8 pieces

140 g (5 oz/1 cup) cherry tomatoes

SALAD

1 cup rocket (arugula)

⅓ cup mint leaves

⅓ cup basil leaves

1 orange, cut into segments

1 tablespoon tahini caesar dressing (page 86)

Spread the pesto onto the pizza base. Add the mozzarella, then cherry tomatoes.

Cook for 5–10 minutes, until the cheese has melted and tomatoes have softened slightly.

Mix the salad ingredients in a bowl and dress with the tahini dressing. Serve pizza with salad on top.

PUMPKIN PIZZA

GF V

2 tablespoons roasted garlic paste

2 tablespoons pumpkin purée

2 bulbs buffalo mozzarella, pulled apart into 8 pieces

1 bunch baby rainbow carrots, cleaned and trimmed

2 avocados, quartered

260 g (9¼ oz/1 cup) ricotta, crumbled

1 teaspoon chilli flakes

Spread the garlic paste then the pumpkin purée onto the pizza base. Add the mozzarella, then baby carrots, avocado, ricotta and chilli flakes.

Cook for 5–10 minutes, until the cheese has melted and other toppings have heated through.

NOTE: If any of the baby carrots are large, cut in half lengthways. Small carrots can be left whole.

FISH FIESTA PIZZA

GF

1 tablespoon tomato paste (concentrated purée)

2 tablespoons roasted garlic paste

2 bulbs buffalo mozzarella, pulled apart into 8 pieces

6 large prawns (shrimp), peeled

70 g (2½ oz/½ cup) cherry tomatoes

½ cup pesto (page 126)

200 g (7 oz) fresh fish, very thinly sliced

Spread the tomato paste and garlic paste onto the pizza base. Add the mozzarella, then the prawns and cherry tomatoes.

Cook for 5–10 minutes, until the prawns are cooked.

Drizzle with pesto. Top with the raw sliced fish, which will delicately be cooked by the heat from the pizza.

Our miso-glazed eggplant is a Japanese flavour mosh pit of soft, sweet, sticky and umami goodness. This is a recipe you might not have thought to cook at home, but it will rock your world and you'll want it every day of the week!

MISO-GLAZED EGGPLANT WITH SOBA NOODLE SALAD

Ⓥ ⒹⒻ ⓋⒺ *Serves 2*

1 large eggplant
1 tablespoon olive oil
2 tablespoons red miso paste
2 tablespoons mirin
1 tablespoon sake
2 teaspoons sugar
2 spring onions (scallions), finely sliced
1 tablespoon sesame seeds

SALAD

80 g (2¾ oz) soba noodles
1 bunch mint, leaves picked
1 bunch coriander, leaves picked
1 bunch radishes, finely sliced
1 orange, segmented

Preheat the oven to 180°C (350°F). Line a baking tray with baking paper.

Cut the eggplant in half lengthways. Using a sharp knife, carefully cut a criss-cross pattern diagonally in the flesh, taking care not to cut through the skin.

Heat the oil in a frying pan over high heat, then add the eggplant halves cut side down. Cook for 3 minutes or until golden. Turn over and cook for 4 minutes, until soft. Transfer to the baking tray, cut side up.

Mix the miso, mirin, sake and sugar to create a paste. Brush the cut surface of the eggplant generously with the paste. Bake for 10 minutes, until the eggplant is cooked and the paste is bubbling.

To make the salad, cook the soba noodles in a large saucepan of boiling water for 4 minutes. Drain into a colander and rinse under cold running water until cool. Drain well. Mix the noodles, mint, coriander, radishes and orange segments in a bowl.

To serve, top the eggplant with the soba noodle salad, and garnish with spring onions and sesame seeds.

I invented this recipe after a sunset surf. By the time I got home it was too late to go shopping and too late to order in, and of course my fridge at home was practically empty — just a few leftover veggies staring back at me.

Bake whatever veggies you have together on a tray with spices, then smash your tomato and let them soak up the hot juices. SO DELISH and a great way to use up the last of the lingering vegetables.

ROASTED SMASHED TOMATO 'SOUP'

Ⓥ *Serves 3—4*

1 sweet potato, diced

2 zucchini (courgette), diced

1 eggplant, diced

1 bunch thyme, leaves picked

1 teaspoon finely grated fresh ginger

3 tablespoons olive oil

1 whole garlic bulb

3 tomatoes

3 baby onions, peeled and halved

1 teaspoon sea salt

½ teaspoon smoked paprika

½ teaspoon cayenne pepper

½ teaspoon ground turmeric

pinch coconut sugar

2 tablespoons chopped parsley leaves

¼ cup pesto (page 126)

crusty bread, to serve

Preheat the oven to 200°C (400°F)

Toss the sweet potato, zucchini, eggplant, thyme, ginger and 1 tablespoon olive oil together, and season with pepper.

Slice the root end of the garlic bulb off.

Pour 1 tablespoon of olive oil into a roasting pan then add the garlic, cut side down.

Score a small cross on the top of each tomato. Place into the roasting pan and add the sweet potato mixture and onions. Drizzle with the remaining olive oil and sprinkle with sea salt, smoked paprika, cayenne pepper, turmeric and coconut sugar.

Bake for 20 minutes, or until the tomatoes are blistered, the garlic has caramelised and all the vegetables are soft.

Transfer the tomatoes to a bowl, and squeeze the roasted garlic flesh over them. Use a fork to mash together well. Stir in the roasted vegetables and parsley.

Serve 'soup' topped with a dollop of pesto, and crusty bread for dipping.

Vegetarian DINNER

An all-vegetarian and gluten-free lasagne packed with mushrooms, eggplant, and zucchini, layered with my vegetarian bolognese and aromatic lemon-herb ricotta, and topped with mixed nuts for some crunch.

ZUCCHINI & EGGPLANT LASAGNE

GF **V** *Serves 5—6*

4 zucchini (courgettes), cut lengthways into 1cm (½ inch) thick slices

2 eggplants, cut lengthways into 1cm (½ inch) thick slices

80 ml (2½ fl oz/⅓ cup) olive oil

520 g (1 lb 2½ oz/2 cups) ricotta

¼ cup basil leaves, finely chopped

¼ cup sage leaves, finely chopped

¼ teaspoon grated nutmeg

finely grated zest of 1 lemon

50 g (1¾ oz/⅓ cup) almonds, finely chopped

45 g (1½ oz/⅓ cup) pistachios, finely chopped

45 g (1½ oz/⅓ cup) macadamia nuts, finely chopped

40 g (1½ oz/⅓ cup) walnuts, finely chopped

100 g (3½ oz/1 cup) grated parmesan cheese

2 cups vegetarian bolognese (page 129)

Preheat the oven to 180°C (350°F). Grease a 20 cm 8 inch) square, 6 cm (2¼ inch) deep ovenproof dish.

Brush the zucchini and eggplant with oil and season with salt and pepper. Heat a large chargrill pan over medium heat and cook the eggplant and zucchini for 4 minutes each side, until tender and golden.

Mix the ricotta, basil, sage, nutmeg and lemon zest together in a bowl until evenly combined. Set aside.

In a separate bowl, mix the nuts and parmesan.

Layer half the eggplant slices over the base of the prepared dish, overlapping to cover completely. Spread the vegetarian bolognese over the eggplant. Use all the zucchini to make a layer over the bolognese, overlapping to cover completely.

Sprinkle half the ricotta mixture over the zucchini, then top with a layer of the remaining eggplant and press down gently. Sprinkle remaining ricotta over, and top with the nut and parmesan mixture.

Bake for 20-25 minutes, and serve hot.

*Simply put: Umami Roast Chicken Heaven!
Roasting the chicken half-submerged in a miso-and-
mushroom broth results in a crispy golden crackling on
the top with slowly poached, tender and juicy flesh in
the middle. Oh, and the FLAVOUR!*

MISO MUSHROOM ROASTED CHICKEN WITH COCONUT & RICE

DF Serves 4—5

1.4 kg (3 lb 2 oz) whole chicken
2 tablespoons olive oil
5 shiitake mushrooms, sliced in half
5 shimeji mushrooms, sliced in half
3 oyster mushrooms, sliced in half
2 garlic cloves, chopped
2 small red chillies, finely chopped
1 cm (½ inch) piece ginger, finely chopped
5 sprigs thyme
finely grated zest of 1 lemon
1 tablespoon miso paste
4 sheets sea spinach (foraged)
  or nori sheets, torn
1 litre (34 fl oz/4 cups) chicken stock
200 g (7 oz/1 cup) jasmine rice
2 nori sheets, extra, torn
125 ml (4 fl oz/½ cup) coconut milk
250 ml (9 fl oz/1 cup) chicken stock, extra
1 bunch coriander (cilantro), chopped

Preheat the oven to 180°C (350°F).

Wipe the chicken dry with paper towel and season with salt and pepper. Heat the oil in a large ovenproof pot over medium heat and add the chicken, breast side down. Cook for about 5 minutes, until browned, then remove and set aside.

Add the mushrooms, garlic, chillies, ginger, thyme and lemon zest. Cook for 4 minutes, stirring occasionally, until tender. Stir in the miso paste, sea spinach or nori and the chicken stock.

Return the chicken to the pot breast side up and bake uncovered for 40–50 minutes, until the chicken is golden and cooked through.

Place the rice into a sieve and wash under cold running water. Drain well, then place into a saucepan with the extra nori, coconut milk and stock. Bring to the boil, then cover with a lid and reduce the heat to low. Cook for 10 minutes or until the rice is tender and has absorbed all the liquid.

Take the pan off the heat and let sit for 20 minutes. Fold through the coriander and serve with the chicken.

Just when you thought curry couldn't get any better, we've Bondi Balanced it — basically, we've put all the ingredients into a pot and into the oven, then we come back and our curry's ready to rock and roll! Thick, creamy and packed with all your favourite spices.

PEANUT & DATE BEEF CURRY

DF *Serves 4—5*

2 tablespoons olive oil

500 g (1 lb 2 oz) chuck steak, cut into 3cm (1¼ inch) pieces

1 onion, finely sliced

60 g (2 oz/¼ cup) green Thai curry paste

400 ml (13½ fl oz) can coconut milk

400 ml (13½ fl oz) chicken stock

1 cm (½ inch) piece lemongrass, bruised

1 tablespoon palm sugar

2 tablespoons peanut butter (page 210)

2 tablespoons fish sauce, plus extra

3 kaffir lime leaves

1 small red chilli, finely chopped

5 chat potatoes, halved

8 pitted dates

1 red capsicum (pepper), sliced

100 g (3½ oz) green beans, trimmed

½ cup coriander (cilantro) leaves, chopped

70 g (2½ oz/½ cup) unsalted roasted peanuts

quinoa or rice, to serve

Preheat the oven to 180°C (350°F).

Heat 1 tablespoon of the oil in a large ovenproof pot over medium heat. Season the meat with salt and pepper, and cook in batches until browned. Set aside.

Heat the remaining oil in the pot and cook the onion until tender. Add the curry paste and cook, stirring, for 20 seconds, until aromatic.

Stir in the coconut milk, chicken stock, lemongrass, palm sugar, peanut butter, fish sauce, lime leaves and chilli. Add the potatoes, dates, capsicum and beef, and bring to a simmer.

Cover the pot tightly with the lid or foil and bake for 1½ hours, or until the beef is tender. Taste and season with a little more fish sauce if you like.

Garnish with beans, coriander and peanuts, and serve with quinoa or rice.

All your favourite seafoods slowly simmered in a flavour-infused broth seasoned to perfection then laid out on the table with toasty bread and epic dipping sauces. What more do we need to say?!

One-Pot
WONDER

SUMMER SEAFOOD BAKE

Serves 4

1 litre (34 fl oz/4 cups) chicken stock
750 ml (26 fl oz/3 cups) white wine
2 bay leaves
pinch saffron threads
6 lemons
4 small kipfler potatoes, scrubbed and halved
1 whole garlic bulb, bashed and broken into cloves
1 small red chilli, finely chopped
4 clams
4 mussels
1 cup seaweed, such as nori, sea lettuce or kombu (optional)
2 onions, diced
2 corn cobs, cleaned and halved crossways
1 bunch thyme, leaves picked
4 scallops, in closed shells
4 prawns (optional), unpeeled
4 oysters (optional), shucked
150 g (5½ oz) butter
⅓ cup parsley leaves, chopped
⅓ cup tarragon leaves, chopped
toasted sourdough, to serve
1 cup macadamia aioli (page 86)

Combine the stock, wine, bay leaves, saffron and 3 halved lemons in a large pot. Bring to the boil over high heat.

Add the potatoes, garlic and chilli. Cover and cook for 3 minutes. Add the clams, mussels, seaweed (if using), onion, corn and thyme and cook for 8–10 minutes, until the corn is tender.

Add the scallops, prawns, oysters (if using), butter, parsley and tarragon. Season with salt and pepper and cook for 5 minutes. Use a slotted spoon to remove all the goodies from the pot and arrange them on a platter or large serving bowl in the middle of the table.

Serve with remaining lemons cut into wedges, and toasted sourdough and aioli.

This chargrilled grass-fed beef rib-eye, topped with my home-made herby chimichurri, is a mouth-watering flavour combination. It's not a new creation, by any means, but it's the perfect illustration of how 'less is more'. Focus on the quality of your ingredients and they will sing with flavour.

DRY AGED BARBECUED ROSEMARY RIB-EYE WITH CHIMICHURRI

DF Serves 4—5

2 x 1 kg (2.2 lb) aged rib-eye steaks (grass-fed)
olive oil, for cooking
1 bunch fresh rosemary
1 quantity chimichurri (page 124)

Take the beef out of the fridge and let it come to room temperature. Preheat the grill plate of a covered BBQ until it is super hot.

Rub the steak with olive oil then season with lots of sea salt. Place onto the hottest part of the BBQ and cook for at least 5 minutes without turning, to create a thick crust. Turn over and cook for 4–5 minutes. Keep flipping and turning every 4–5 minutes for about 20 minutes in total, to create a thick crust.

Move the steak to the flat plate (unlit side of the BBQ), close lid and cook for another 10–15 minutes.

Place half the bunch of rosemary onto a large sheet of foil. Sit the steaks on the rosemary, drizzle with more oil and season with more salt. Top with the rest of the rosemary then fold the foil over to tightly enclose. Wrap in a damp tea towel and let rest for 10 minutes.

Remove, slice and serve with chimichurri.

This recipe takes the simple pork chop to another level. Tender, organic pork glazed and topped with sweet-and-sour caramelised apples on a bed of polenta. YUM!

PORK CHOPS WITH SWEET & SOUR APPLES & POLENTA

GF Serves 4

2 tablespoons olive oil

4 thick pork chops

4 apples, quartered and cored

1 cinnamon stick

1 tablespoon brown sugar

80 g (2¾ oz) butter

3 sprigs thyme

1 tablespoon apple cider vinegar

375 ml (13 fl oz/1½ cups) vegetable stock

1 bunch thyme

4 sprigs rosemary

1 bay leaf

1 lemon myrtle leaf

1 garlic clove, bruised

85 g (3 oz/½ cup) fine polenta

50 g (1¾ oz) butter

50 g (1¾ oz) parmesan cheese, grated

2 tablespoons pomegranate seeds

Heat the oil in a large frying pan over medium-high heat. Season the pork with salt and pepper and cook for 4 minutes on each side until coloured and cooked through. Transfer to a large plate to rest.

Add the apples, cinnamon, sugar, butter and thyme sprigs to the pan and cook until the apples are coloured and soft. Deglaze with apple cider vinegar then pour over the pork chops. Keep warm.

Place the stock into a saucepan and add the herbs and garlic. Slowly bring to a simmer over medium-low heat, to infuse the flavours. Remove the herbs and garlic. Add the polenta and cook, stirring, for 6 minutes or until thick. Stir in the butter and parmesan and season with salt and pepper.

Serve the polenta topped with the pork and caramelised apples, sprinkled with pomegranate seeds.

Spend less time alone at the BBQ and more time with your mates, with our salsa verde baked salmon. A one-tray wonder that just goes straight into the oven ... it's that simple! Lean, summer-inspired fresh flavours.

SALSA VERDE BAKED SALMON

GF DF *Serves 4*

60 ml (2 fl oz/¼ cup) olive oil

⅓ onion, diced

½ fennel bulb, diced

3 garlic cloves, minced

1 small red chilli, finely chopped

1 teaspoon ground turmeric

200 g (7 oz/1 cup) buckwheat

500 ml (17 fl oz/2 cups) chicken stock

finely grated zest of 1 lemon

finely grated zest of 1 orange

100 g (3½ oz) snow peas, trimmed

50 g (1¾ oz) green beans, trimmed

100 g (3½ oz) asparagus, trimmed

3 yellow patty pan squash, cut into 4 cm (1½ inch) chunks

1 lemon, zest finely grated, sliced

½ cup salsa verde (page 217)

4 x 200 g salmon fillets

1 iceberg lettuce, broken into cups

Preheat the oven to 200°C (400°F).

Heat the olive oil in a saucepan over medium heat. Add the onion, fennel, garlic and chilli and cook for 6–7 minutes, until tender. Add the turmeric and cook for 20 seconds, until fragrant.

Add the buckwheat, stirring constantly until the grains are coated and translucent. Add the stock and bring to the boil. Reduce the heat to low and cook uncovered for 15–20 minutes, until the buckwheat is tender and all the liquid has been absorbed.

Take the pot off the heat and stir in the lemon and orange zest. Cover with a lid and let sit for about 12 minutes.

In a mixing bowl toss the snow peas, beans, asparagus, squash, lemon zest and slices and two-thirds of the salsa verde. Transfer the mixture to a 20 cm (8 inch) square, 6 cm (2½ inch) deep ovenproof dish.

Season the salmon fillets with salt and pepper and place on top of vegetables. Dress the salmon with the remaining salsa verde, and bake for 20–25 minutes until golden and the salmon flesh flakes easily.

Serve the salmon with the lettuce cups and the buckwheat.

If you're after a recipe to impress your mates, I promise you these are pork tacos like you've never seen (or eaten) before! Barbequed to perfection with my (no-longer) secret whole chargrilled pineapple and avocado salsa.

PORK & PINEAPPLE TACOS

DF Serves 6—7

2 kg (4 lb 8 oz) piece pork belly, rind removed
24 soft corn tortillas, warmed

CURING MIX
290 g (10 oz/1 cup) sea salt
220 g (8 oz/1 cup) sugar
2 lemon myrtle leaves
finely grated zest of 1 lemon
finely grated zest of 1 orange
finely grated zest of 1 lime
3 garlic cloves, minced
1 small red chilli, finely chopped
1 tablespoon ground black pepper
1 teaspoon fennel seeds

MOJO MARINADE
½ cup coriander (cilantro) leaves, chopped
juice of 2 lemons
juice of 2 oranges
juice of 3 limes
½ cup mint leaves, chopped
2 garlic cloves, minced
1 teaspoon ground cumin
1 small red chilli, finely chopped
125 ml (4 fl oz/½ cup) olive oil

SALSA
1 pineapple, kept whole but skin removed
1 garlic clove, minced
1 small red chilli, finely chopped
1 red capsicum (pepper), diced
1 red onion, diced
2 avocados, diced
4 tomatoes, diced
½ cup mint leaves

For the curing mix, combine all the ingredients in a shallow non-metallic dish. Add the pork belly and massage with the curing mix until it's completely covered. Place in the fridge for 12 hours.

Wash under cold water to remove the curing mix then return the pork to the cleaned dish.

For the marinade, mix the coriander, citrus juices, mint, garlic, cumin, chilli and olive oil and pour over the pork. Refrigerate for another 12 hours.

Preheat the BBQ grill plate to medium heat. Take the pork from the marinade and pat dry with paper towel. Place onto the BBQ and cook for 50–60 minutes, turning and moving every 5 minutes to create an even caramelised crust.

When the pork begins to flake and fall apart remove from the BBQ. Wrap it in foil and then a damp clean tea towel and let it rest for 30 minutes before carving.

For the salsa, place the whole pineapple onto the BBQ and cook for 20 minutes, constantly moving and turning until soft and caramelised on all sides. Cool slightly then dice into 1cm (½ inch) cubes. Mix the pineapple, garlic, chilli, capsicum, onion, avocado, tomato and mint together. Season with salt and pepper.

Heat the tortillas. Serve the pork and salsa wrapped in the warm tortillas.

NOTE: You can leave out the curing part of the recipe to save time, if you prefer, though it does add great flavour.

BALANCE TIP #4
SLEEP ROUTINE

Your body works off an internal body clock and, like all clocks, it will only work if it runs on time! One of the best ways to ensure a solid sleep is to stick to a sleep routine.

Sleep is when your body repairs, grows and recovers both mentally and physically from your often hectic day-to-day schedule.

It's time to get into some good habits: set up your nest, eat right and sleep well.

- **Bedtime:** To help fall into a rhythm, try setting a bedtime routine. This will help your brain regulate your serotonin and melatonin levels throughout the day, meaning that when bedtime approaches your brain will know it's time to start powering down.

- **Caffeine Clock:** At Bondi Harvest, we are definitely not against coffee, tea or chocolate! However, if you want to fall asleep easily, avoid those heavy caffeine hits after 3 pm. You'll see an increase in your sleep quality in no time.

- **Light & Dark:** Light pollution doesn't just impact your view of the stars; it's also affecting your sleep quality. To avoid confusing your body clock, keep your room dark with block-out curtains and leave the blue-light, brain-stimulating electronics out of the bedroom.

SLEEP FOODS

Sleep is controlled by your body through different hormones, monoamines, minerals and vitamins, and what you're eating can have a direct impact on your sleep quality. Here are our top foods to help you get to sleep.

- **Chickpeas & Fish:** High in vitamin B6, chickpeas and fish (particularly salmon, halibut and tuna) help your body to create melatonin, that all-important sleep hormone.

- **Almonds, Kale & Spinach:** Almonds are high in magnesium, a mineral important to improving sleep quality. Green, leafy vegetables like kale and spinach are high in calcium, which aids the brain in producing tryptophan, important in the manufacture of melatonin.

- **Chamomile Tea:** Not only does it have an amazing aroma and taste, chamomile tea is also shown to increase glycine levels, which acts as a muscle and nerve relaxant. So try brewing a cup before bedtime to lull your mind and body into a state of relaxation.

Balance means not missing out on the good stuff and not feeling guilty when dessert time rolls around. We believe if you're *vibeing* chocolate cake, then get your cake on. If you're after something a little lighter, we've got that covered too.

BAKED DESSERTS 174

Some of my happiest moments in the kitchen have been while baking. There's something so satisfying and nostalgic about baking—every step done with purpose, from sifting the flour to patiently waiting for the cake to cool before you turn it out.

FRUIT ICE-CREAM WHIPS 182

So smooth, rich and delicious, it's hard to believe these fruit ice-cream whips are healthy and free of refined sugar. Using frozen fruit as a base, we've then elevated and 'chefified' the flavour combinations—they're so tasty, it's hard to believe they're also good for you!

ICE BLOCKS 186

These ice blocks are the ultimate summer treats or post-workout snack. They're 100% flavour-filled pure wholefood goodness. And just when you thought they're as yummy as it gets, we've added a few ridiculously delicious toppings to dip them in to.

RAW & FRUITY 192

This section's about keeping it raw, fresh and as natural as possible to create decadent desserts. You'll be asking yourself how something made from nuts and fruit can be so damn tasty and rich. These recipes are the ideal guilt-free treat for when you're feeling like something a little sweet.

LOAVES 200

Sweet or savoury and perfect for breakfast, a mid-afternoon nibble or dessert, these epic loaves are the ultimate wholefood treat.

BAKED DONUTS

Ⓥ *Makes 10*

5 Medjool dates, pitted

60 g (2 oz) soft butter

60 ml (2 fl oz/¼ cup) coconut oil

75 g (2½ oz/½ cup) coconut sugar

1 vanilla bean, split, seeds scraped

2 eggs

1 teaspoon ground cinnamon

2 teaspoons baking powder

¼ teaspoon bicarbonate of soda (baking soda)

¼ teaspoon sea salt

250 ml (9 fl oz/1 cup) coconut milk

480 g (1 lb 1 oz/3 cups) wholemeal plain (all-purpose) flour

2 cups fruit ice cream whips (page 183)

1 cup ice-block topping (page 189)

Preheat the oven to 200°C (400°F). Grease ten 125 ml (4 fl oz/½ cup) capacity donut pans.

Soak dates in boiling water for 5 minutes, then drain and purée until smooth.

Use electric beaters to beat the butter, oil and sugar until smooth and fluffy. Add the date purée and vanilla seeds, then the eggs one at a time, beating well after each addition.

Fold the cinnamon, baking powder, bicarb and salt through, then the milk. Sift the flour over and add the husks, then fold through until combined and smooth.

Spoon the batter into donut pans. Bake for 10 minutes, until risen and golden brown. Cool in the pans for 10–15 minutes then transfer to a wire rack to cool completely.

Once cooled slice in half and fill with your choice of fruit ice cream whip, and top with your choice of toppings.

VARIATIONS

CHOCOLATE: Add 1 tablespoon 100% raw cacao powder and 2 teaspoons cocoa nibs to the batter.

BLUEBERRY SWIRL: Add 1 tablespoon mashed blueberries, 1 tablespoon berry jam and finely grated zest of 1 lemon to the batter.

TURMERIC LEMON: Add 2 teaspoons ground turmeric, finely grated zest of 2 lemons and 2 tablespoons honey to the batter.

CHOCOLATE, CHILLI & SEASONAL FRUIT TART

Ⓥ Serves 4—5

2 sheets frozen puff pastry, thawed slightly

1 egg, lightly beaten

160 g (5½ oz/½ cup) marmalade

500 g (1 lb 2 oz) seasonal fruit
(mango, berries, banana, star fruit)

2 tablespoons coconut flakes, toasted

CHOCOLATE CHILLI CREAM

500 ml (17 fl oz/2 cups) milk

½ vanilla bean, split, seeds scraped

2 teaspoons 100% raw cacao powder

½ teaspoon cayenne pepper

2 eggs

100 g (3½ oz) coconut sugar or honey

35 g (1¼ oz) cornflour (cornstarch)

100 g (3½ oz) dark chocolate, chopped

60 g (2 oz) butter, chopped

Preheat the oven to 200°C (400°F). Line a large baking tray with baking paper.

To make the chocolate chilli cream, combine the milk, vanilla seeds, cacao powder and cayenne pepper in a saucepan and heat until simmering.

Whisk the eggs, sugar and cornflour in a mixing bowl until smooth. Pour half the hot milk mixture onto the egg mixture, whisking constantly. Pour back into the saucepan with the remaining milk.

Whisk over low heat until the mixture thickens (do not allow to boil). Stir in the chocolate until melted and smooth. Remove from the heat and whisk in the butter. Transfer to a bowl, cover and refrigerate until cool.

Cut the centre out of one of the pastry sheets, leaving a 3 cm (1¼ inch) square frame. Place the other pastry sheet onto the lined baking tray. Use a fork to prick the pastry all over with lots of little dimples. Brush the pastry with egg, and carefully place the cut pastry frame on top, lining up the edges. Brush the frame with egg.

Bake for 10–15 minutes, until puffed and golden brown. Set aside to cool completely.

Smear the pastry base with marmalade, then spoon or pipe the chocolate chilli cream on top to cover. Arrange the seasonal fruit on top, sprinkle with coconut and serve.

HEALTHY PAVLOVAS

 Serves 8

185 g (6½ oz/1¼ cups) coconut sugar
4 egg whites
1 vanilla bean, split, seeds scraped
finely grated zest of 1 lemon
1 teaspoon lemon juice
2 teaspoons cornflour (cornstarch)
coconut yoghurt and seasonal fruit, to serve

Preheat the oven to 150°C (300°F). Line 2 large baking trays with baking paper.

Place the sugar into a food processor and pulse several times so that it has a finer texture.

Use electric beaters to beat the egg whites until stiff peaks form. Add the sugar 1 tablespoon at a time, beating until dissolved between each addition. Beat until thick and glossy, then add the vanilla seeds, lemon zest, juice and cornflour. Beat briefly until combined.

Spread the mixture into eight 8 cm (3 inch) circles on the baking trays. Bake for one hour or until crisp on the outside. Cool on the trays for 30 minutes, then carefully transfer to a wire rack to cool completely.

Serve topped with coconut yoghurt and seasonal fruit.

RICOTTA CHOCOLATE CAKE

(V) Serves 6

90 g (3 oz) dark chocolate
   (minimum 85% cocoa), chopped
60 g (2 oz) butter, chopped
300 g (10½ oz) ricotta, crumbled
finely grated zest of 1 lemon
75 g (2½ oz/½ cup) coconut sugar
2 eggs
180 ml (6 fl oz/¾ cup) coconut milk
200 g (7 oz/2 cups) almond meal
25 g (¾ oz/¼ cup) 100% raw cacao powder
2 teaspoons baking powder
3 tablespoons cocoa nibs
80 g (2¾ oz/½ cup) raspberries
3 tablespoons coconut flakes

TOPPING

200 g (7 oz/2 cups) 100% raw cacao powder
250 ml (9 fl oz/1 cup) coconut oil
2 tablespoons maple syrup
1 mango, sliced
125 g (4½ oz/1 cup) raspberries or blueberries
1 tablespoon shredded coconut

Preheat oven 180°C (350°F). Grease a 20 cm (8 inch) springform tin and line the base with baking paper.

Combine the chocolate and butter in a double boiler or a heatproof bowl over a saucepan of simmering water. Melt gently over low heat (make sure the bottom of the bowl doesn't touch the water) and stir until smooth. Set aside to cool to room temperature.

Use electric beaters to beat the ricotta, lemon zest, sugar and eggs in a large bowl until light and creamy. Fold the melted chocolate mixture and milk through until evenly combined. Add the almond meal, cacao powder, baking powder and cocoa nibs and fold through until combined, then fold in the raspberries.

Transfer mixture to the prepared tin. Sprinkle with coconut flakes and bake for 25–30 minutes or until firm to the touch and a skewer comes out clean. Let the cake cool for 20 minutes before removing from the tin and adding the topping.

To make the topping, mix the cacao powder, coconut oil and maple syrup in a bowl or large jug. Pour over the cake. Garnish with fresh fruit and shredded coconut.

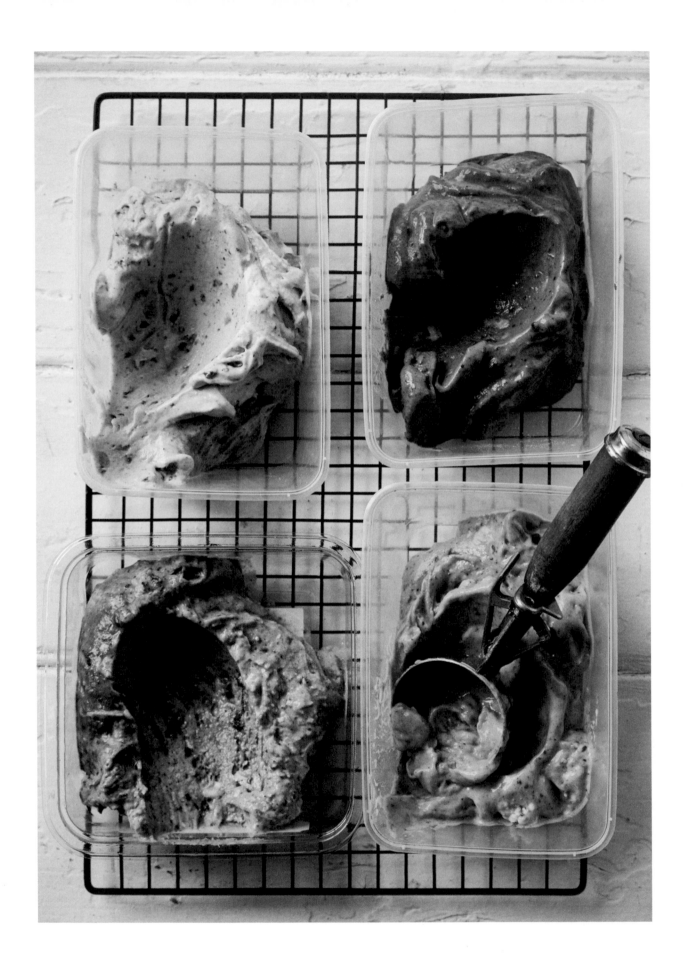

FRUIT ICE CREAM WHIPS

BANANA STRAWBERRY ICE CREAM

GF **V** Serves 2–3

2 frozen peeled and chopped bananas
70 g (2½ oz/½ cup) chopped frozen strawberries
2 tablespoons strawberry jam
1 tablespoon vanilla yoghurt

Place the food processor bowl into the freezer for at least 1 hour before starting.

Place all the ingredients into the food processor, turn on high and process until smooth. Transfer into an airtight container and freeze for 5 minutes before eating.

NOTE: It is easier to peel and chop fresh bananas, then freeze them in a snap lock bag (with the air expelled).

PEANUT CRUNCH ICE CREAM

GF **V** Serves 2–3

3 frozen peeled and chopped bananas
2 tablespoons peanut butter
1 tablespoon vanilla yoghurt
2 teaspoons maple syrup
2 tablespoons cocoa nibs

Place food processor bowl into the freezer for at least 1 hour before starting.

Place all the ingredients except the cocoa nibs into the food processor, turn on high and process until smooth. Add the cocoa nibs and pulse until combined.

Transfer into an airtight container and freeze for 5 minutes before eating.

CHOCOLATE COFFEE BANANA ICE CREAM

GF **V** Serves 2–3

3 frozen peeled and chopped bananas
1½ tablespoons 100% raw cacao powder
1 tablespoon toasted coffee beans, crushed in a mortar and pestle
1 tablespoon vanilla coconut yoghurt
2 teaspoons coconut sugar

Place the food processor bowl into the freezer for at least 1 hour before starting.

Place all the ingredients into the food processor, turn on high and process until smooth. Transfer into an airtight container and freeze for 5 minutes before eating.

DATE, SALTED CARAMEL, SESAME & HAZELNUT ICE CREAM

GF **V** **DF** **VE** Serves 2–3

3 frozen peeled and chopped bananas
2 Medjool dates, pitted
2 tablespoons hazelnuts, toasted
1 tablespoon homemade tahini (page 218)
1 tablespoon sesame seeds
2 pinches sea salt

Place the food processor bowl into the freezer for at least 1 hour before starting.

Place all the ingredients except the sesame seeds and salt into the food processor, turn on high and process until smooth. Add the sesame seeds and salt and pulse until combined.

Transfer into an airtight container and freeze for 5 minutes before eating.

ICE BLOCKS

TRIPLE COCONUT POPSICLES

GF V DF VE Makes 4

200 ml (7 fl oz) coconut milk
2 tablespoons coconut sugar
finely grated zest of 1 lemon
finely grated zest of 1 lime
200 ml (7 fl oz) coconut water
2 tablespoons shredded coconut

Place the coconut milk, coconut sugar, lemon and lime zest into a blender and blend until smooth. Divide half the mixture between four 100 ml (3½ fl oz) ice block moulds. Freeze for 2 hours, inserting the sticks when the mixture is starting to become firm.

Once frozen, add the coconut water and shredded coconut to the moulds, dividing evenly. Freeze for 2 hours, until frozen.

Top with the remaining coconut milk mixture. Freeze for 2 hours or until firm.

MANGO & RASPBERRY LASSI POPS

GF V  Makes 4

1 large mango, flesh chopped
½ teaspoon ground turmeric
¼ teaspoon cayenne pepper
1 tablespoon honey or maple syrup
12 raspberries
260 g (9¼ oz/1 cup) coconut yoghurt

Place the mango, turmeric, cayenne and honey into a high-powered blender and blitz until smooth.

Pour half the mixture into four 100 ml (3½ fl oz) ice-block moulds, dividing evenly. Freeze for 2 hours, inserting the sticks when the mixture is starting to become firm.

Once frozen, place three raspberries on top of frozen mango purée and cover with coconut yoghurt. Freeze for another 2 hours, then pour in the remaining mango and freeze for 2 hours or until firm.

BERRY KOMBUCHA CHIA SEED POPS

GF V DF VE Makes 4

250 ml (9 fl oz/1 cup) orange juice
60 ml (2 fl oz/¼ cup) kombucha
50 g (1¾ oz/⅓ cup) mixed berries (fresh or frozen)
1 tablespoon maple syrup
1 tablespoon chia seeds
1 teaspoon thyme leaves
4 mint leaves

Place all the ingredients into a blender and blend until smooth. Divide the mixture between four 100 ml (3½ fl oz) ice-block moulds.

Freeze for at least 5 hours, inserting the sticks when the mixture is starting to become firm.

RED VELVET POPSICLES

GF V DF VE Makes 4

430 ml (14½ fl oz/1¾ cups) coconut milk
40 g (1½ oz/¼ cup) chia seeds
25 g (¾ oz/¼ cup) 100% raw cacao powder
2 tablespoons maple syrup
2 teaspoons beetroot juice
pinch sea salt

Place all the ingredients into a blender and blend until smooth. Divide the mixture between four 100 ml (3½ fl oz) ice-block moulds.

Freeze for at least 5 hours, inserting the sticks when the mixture is starting to become firm.

Place all the ingredients into a blender and blend until smooth. Divide the mixture between four 100 ml (3½ fl oz) ice-block moulds.

Freeze for at least 5 hours, inserting the sticks when the mixture is starting to become firm.

HONEY, COCONUT & SEASONAL FRUIT POPS

GF V DF Makes 4

1 tablespoon honey
4 strawberries
4 raspberries
4 blueberries
4 grapes
4 mint sprigs
300 ml (10 fl oz) coconut water

Lightly mix the honey and fruit together, and evenly distribute between four 100 ml (3½ fl oz) ice-block moulds along with the mint. Fill with coconut water. Freeze for at least 5 hours, inserting the sticks when the mixture is starting to become firm.

DARK CHOCOLATE POPSICLES

GF V DF VE Makes 4

125 ml (4 fl oz/½ cup) coconut milk
60 ml (2 fl oz/¼ cup) maple syrup
2 ripe avocados, flesh scooped out
50 g (1¾ oz/½ cup) 100% raw cacao powder
2 tablespoons cocoa nibs
1 teaspoon vanilla extract

ICE BLOCK TOPPINGS

BLUEBERRY YOGHURT TOPPING

GF V Serves 4—5

520 g (1 lb 2½ oz/2 cups) yoghurt
2 tablespoons coconut oil
90 g (3 oz/⅓ cup) blueberries, fresh or frozen
1 cup Bondi Harvest granola (page 214)

Line a tray with baking paper and place into the freezer. Place the yoghurt, coconut oil and blueberries into a blender and blend until smooth and combined.

Dip frozen popsicles into the mixture, garnish with granola then place onto the tray and freeze for 30 minutes before eating.

COCONUT & ALMOND TOPPING

GF V DF VE Serves 4—5

250 ml (9 fl oz/1 cup) coconut cream
125 ml (4 fl oz/½ cup) coconut oil
60 ml (2 fl oz/¼ cup) maple syrup
2 tablespoons almond meal
1 tablespoon coconut flakes
1 tablespoon flaked almonds
1 tablespoon cocoa nibs

Line a tray with baking paper and place into the freezer. Place the coconut cream, coconut oil, maple syrup and almond meal into a blender or bowl and blend or whisk until combined.

Drizzle over the frozen popsicles (or dip them into the mixture) and garnish with coconut flakes, almonds and cocoa nibs. Place onto the tray and freeze for 30 minutes before eating.

MATCHA, HONEY, LEMON & TARRAGON TOPPING

GF V DF Serves 4—5

60 ml (2 fl oz/¼ cup) coconut oil
80 ml (2½ fl oz/⅓ cup) honey
50 g (1¾ oz/⅓ cup) sesame seeds
1 tablespoon matcha powder
shredded zest of 2 lemons
2 tablespoons chopped tarragon

Line a tray with baking paper and place into the freezer. Place the coconut oil, honey, sesame seeds and matcha powder into a blender or bowl and blend or whisk until combined.

Drizzle over the frozen popsicles and top with lemon zest and tarragon. Place onto the tray and freeze for 30 minutes before eating.

PEANUT TAHINI CARAMEL TOPPING

GF V DF VE Serves 4—5

135 g (4¾ oz/½ cup) homemade tahini (page 218)
2 Medjool dates, pitted
1 tablespoon almond milk
35 g (1¼ oz/¼ cup) chopped peanuts
1 teaspoon sea salt

Line a tray with baking paper and place into the freezer. Place the tahini, dates and almond milk into a blender and blend until combined.

Drizzle over the frozen popsicles (or dip them into the mixture) and top with peanuts and a pinch of sea salt. Place onto the tray and freeze for 30 minutes before eating.

RAW & FRUITY

BRULEE CITRUS

(GF) (V) Serves 6

3 ruby grapefruits, halved
3 oranges, halved
3 lemons, halved
225 g (8 oz/1½ cups) coconut sugar
260 g (9¼ oz/1 cup) coconut yoghurt
½ cup mint leaves, chopped
80 g (2¾ oz/½ cup) almonds, chopped

Trim the base off each piece of citrus to stabilise the fruit and prevent it from rocking around.

Place the fruit, cut side down, onto paper towels and leave for 10 minutes to dry. Invert fruit and sprinkle evenly with 1 tablespoon of the sugar.

Using a kitchen torch, heat the sugar until melted and beginning to turn a dark amber colour.

Garnish with yoghurt, mint and almonds.

TEQUILA-DRUNKEN BAKED FRUIT

(V) Serves 6

1 kg (2 lb 4 oz) seasonal fruit
80 ml (2½ fl oz/⅓ cup) honey
1 tablespoon shredded coconut
2 vanilla beans, split, seeds scraped
1 stick lemongrass, bashed
2 kaffir lime or lemon myrtle leaves
finely grated zest of 2 oranges, juice of 1
finely grated zest of 3 lemons, juice of 1
2 cm piece (¾ inch) piece ginger, finely grated
125 ml (4 fl oz/½ cup) tequila
260 g (9¼ oz/1 cup) ricotta
1 tablespoon finely chopped mint
6 fresh baked scones, to serve

Preheat the oven to 200°C (400°F) and line a large rimmed baking tray with baking paper.

Place the fruit, honey, coconut, vanilla seeds, lemongrass, kaffir lime leaves, zest and ginger into a large mixing bowl. Toss to combine, then arrange in a single layer on the tray.

Bake for 20–25 minutes, until the fruit is very soft and caramelised. Deglaze with tequila, orange and lemon juice. Cool to room temperature.

Combine the ricotta and mint. Serve the fruit and ricotta on the warm scones.

RAW CARROT CAKE WITH MATCHA ICING

GF **V** **DF** **VE** *Serves 6*

300 g (10½ oz/2 cups) grated carrot
180 g (6½ oz/1 cup) Medjool dates, pitted
1 tablespoon coconut oil
70 g (2½ oz/½ cup) macadamia nuts
60 g (2 oz/½ cup) walnuts
finely grated zest of 1 orange
1 teaspoon ground cinnamon
⅓ teaspoon finely grated fresh ginger
¼ teaspoon ground nutmeg
1 vanilla bean, split, seeds scraped
90 g (3 oz/¾ cup) goji berries

MATCHA ICING

1 avocado
1 tablespoon maple syrup
finely grated zest and juice of 1 lemon
1 tablespoon matcha powder
1 tablespoon coconut oil

Line a 20 cm (8 inch) round cake tin or flan tin with baking paper.

Wrap carrot in a clean tea towel and then twist to squeeze out any excess liquid.

Combine dates, coconut oil, macadamia nuts and walnuts in a food processor and process until crumbly and combined.

Add the carrot, orange zest, cinnamon, ginger, nutmeg and vanilla seeds. Continue to process until a smooth dough forms. Fold the goji berries through. Spoon into prepared tin and place in the fridge for 20 minutes to set.

To make the matcha icing, scoop the avocado flesh into a food processor and add the maple syrup, lemon zest, juice, matcha powder and coconut oil. Process until smooth. Spoon and spread on top of the cake and serve.

TIP: For simple grab-and-go mini carrot cakes, use muffin tins instead.

RUM LAVENDER CHOCOLATE BROWNIES

GF V DF *Serves 9*

270 g (9½ oz/1½ cups) Medjool dates, pitted
90 ml (3 fl oz) spiced rum
80 g (2¾ oz/½ cup) hemp seeds
100 g (3½ oz/1 cup) almond meal
50 g (1¾ oz/½ cup) 100% raw cacao powder
1 vanilla bean, split, seeds scraped
finely grated zest of 1 lemon
2 tablespoons chopped macadamias
2 tablespoons cocoa nibs

TOPPING

125 ml (4 fl oz/½ cup) coconut oil
½ teaspoon finely chopped lavender leaves
50 g (1¾ oz/½ cup) 100% raw cacao powder
2 tablespoons maple syrup
1 tablespoon bee pollen (optional)
5 lavender flowers or rose petals (optional)

Line a 20 cm (8 inch) square cake tin with baking paper.

Soak the dates in the spiced rum for at least 10 minutes, then place into a food processor with the hemp seeds and process until puréed and combined.

Add the almond meal, cacao, vanilla seeds and lemon zest. Process until combined and sticky. Transfer to a bowl and fold through the macadamias and cocoa nibs.

Spoon into the prepared tin and smooth the surface. Refrigerate for at least 2 hours, until firm, or place into the freezer for 15 minutes if you're short on time.

To make the topping, gently heat the coconut oil with the lavender in a saucepan, then remove from the heat and set aside for 5 minutes to infuse. Sift in cacao powder then add the maple syrup and mix until combined and smooth.

Pour the topping onto the brownie slab and refrigerate for 10 minutes. Cut into squares to serve. Garnish with a sprinkle of bee pollen and some fresh lavender flowers or rose petals, if using.

EPIC PANNA COTTA
WITH WATERMELON GRANITA

GF Serves 4—6

70 g (2½ oz/½ cup) chopped pistachios
¼ cup chopped mint leaves

PANNA COTTA
600 ml (21 fl oz) milk
3 tablespoons shredded coconut
2 vanilla beans, split, seeds scraped
finely grated zest of 1 lemon
75 g (2½ oz) sugar or honey
2 teaspoons gelatine powder
200 g (7 oz) Greek or homemade yoghurt
 (page 216)

GRANITA
700 g (1½ lbs/5 cups) cubed seedless
 watermelon
165 g (5¾ oz/¾ cup) sugar
finely grated zest and juice of 1 lemon
2 tablespoons shredded coconut
2 tablespoons pomegranate seeds
1 tablespoon chopped mint

To make the panna cotta, combine the milk, coconut, vanilla beans and seeds, lemon zest and sugar (or honey). Warm (don't boil) on a low heat for 15 minutes, then strain.

Combine the gelatine and 2 tablespoons warm water and mix well until combined. While the milk is still warm, add gelatine mixture and stir to dissolve.

Strain once more and then let cool until room temperature. Fold the yoghurt through and pour into a 4-cup capacity shallow serving dish. Refrigerate overnight, or until set.

For the granita, place watermelon, sugar, lemon zest and juice in a blender and process until combined. Pour into a flat baking tray then mix in the coconut, pomegranate seeds and mint. Freeze for 2 hours, then take out and use the back of a fork to mix, scrape and bash any frozen parts.

Place back into the freezer and freeze for another 2 hours. Repeat the mashing process. Wrap with plastic or foil and keep in the freezer until needed.

To serve, top panna cotta with granita. Sprinkle with strawberries and mint, and serve immediately.

NOTE: To cool the panna cotta mixture quickly, pour into a metal bowl and set over a larger bowl filled with ice cubes. Stir to release the heat. When cold, pour into dish and place into fridge to set.

LOAVES

BANANA, GINGER & COCONUT LOAF

V Makes 1 loaf

1 tablespoon butter, melted, for greasing
2 bananas
finely grated zest of 1 lemon
1 teaspoon finely grated fresh ginger
200 ml (7 fl oz) coconut oil
2 eggs, lightly beaten
480 g (1 lb 1 oz/3 cups) wholemeal plain
   (all-purpose) flour
2 teaspoons bicarbonate of soda
200 g (7 oz/1⅓ cups) coconut sugar
60 g (2 oz/½ cup) walnuts
35 g (1¼ oz/½ cup) shredded coconut
½ teaspoon salt

Preheat the oven to 180°C (350°F). Grease a 21 x 11 cm (8½ x 4½ inch) loaf pan with melted butter.

Mash the bananas in a bowl, then mix in the lemon zest, ginger, coconut oil and eggs. Combine the flour, bicarb, coconut sugar, walnuts, shredded coconut and salt in a separate bowl. Gently fold the wet mixture through the dry ingredients until combined and smooth, adding up to 1 tablespoon of water if it is a little dry.

Transfer the batter to the prepared loaf pan and bake for 1–1½ hours, until golden on top and a skewer inserted into the centre of the loaf comes out clean.

Cool in the tin for 10 minutes, then turn out onto a wire rack to cool.

BEETROOT, CAYENNE, THYME & GOAT'S CHEESE LOAF

V Makes 1 loaf

1 tablespoon butter, melted, for greasing
400 g (14 oz/2½ cups) wholemeal plain
   (all-purpose) flour
1 tablespoon baking powder
1 teaspoon coarsely ground black pepper
1 teaspoon salt
1 teaspoon cayenne pepper
2 eggs, lightly beaten
80 ml (2½ fl oz/⅓ cup) extra virgin olive oil
130 g (4½ oz/½ cup) Greek or homemade yoghurt
   (page 216)
225 g (8 oz/1½ cups) shredded beetroot (red or yellow)
50 g (1¾ oz/½ cup) grated parmesan cheese
120 g goat's cheese, crumbled
2 tablespoons chopped parsley leaves
1 teaspoon fresh thyme leaves
finely grated zest of 1 lemon

Preheat the oven to 180°C (350°F). Grease a 21 x 11 cm (8½ x 4½ inch) loaf pan with butter.

Combine the flour, baking powder, pepper, salt and cayenne pepper in a mixing bowl. Using your hands, a whisk or the back of a spoon, break up any lumps and mix together well.

In another bowl, mix the eggs, olive oil, yoghurt, beetroot, parmesan, goat's cheese, herbs and lemon zest together until evenly combined. Using a spatula, gently fold the dry ingredients into the wet mixture until the batter comes together. Transfer batter to the prepared loaf pan and bake for 40–50 minutes, until golden on top and a skewer inserted into the centre of the loaf comes out clean.

Cool in the tin for 10 minutes, then turn out onto a wire rack to cool.

CHAI-SPICED POACHED PEAR LOAF

(V) Makes 1 loaf

1 tablespoon butter, melted, for greasing
2 tablespoons honey
1 tablespoon chai tea leaves
2 firm pears, peeled but kept whole
2 bananas
finely grated zest of 1 lemon
1 teaspoon finely grated fresh ginger
200 ml (7 fl oz) coconut oil
2 eggs, lightly beaten
480 g (1 lb 1 oz/3 cups) wholemeal plain
  (all-purpose) flour
2 teaspoons bicarbonate of soda (baking soda)
½ teaspoon ground cinnamon
⅓ teaspoon grated fresh nutmeg
½ teaspoon salt
200 g (7 oz/1⅓ cups) coconut sugar
160 g (5 ½ oz/1 cup) almonds, chopped

Preheat the oven to 180°C (350°F). Grease a 21 x 11 cm (8½ x 4½ inch) loaf pan with melted butter.

Combine 1 litre (34 fl oz/4 cups) water, honey and chai tea leaves in a saucepan large enough to fit the pears. Bring to a simmer. Add the pears, cover and cook on a low heat for 15–20 minutes or until the pears are soft. Remove pears from the poaching liquid and refrigerate until cold.

Mash the bananas in a bowl, then mix in the lemon zest, ginger, coconut oil and eggs. Combine the flour, bicarb, cinnamon, nutmeg, salt, coconut sugar and almonds. Gently fold the wet mixture through the dry ingredients until combined and smooth, adding up to 2 tablespoons of water if it is a little dry.

Transfer half the batter to the prepared loaf pan, then stand the pears in the batter. Add remaining batter to the pan. Cover pan with foil.

Bake for 1½ hours then remove foil and cook for another hour, until golden on top and a skewer inserted into the centre of the loaf comes out clean.

Cool in the tin for 10 minutes, then turn out onto a wire rack to cool.

ZUCCHINI, TURMERIC & GOJI LOAF

(V) Makes 1 loaf

1 tablespoon butter, melted, for greasing
400 g (14 oz/2½ cups) wholemeal plain
  (all-purpose) flour
3 teaspoons baking powder
1 teaspoon ground black pepper
1½ teaspoons salt
1 teaspoon ground turmeric
1 tablespoon goji berries
2 eggs, lightly beaten
80 ml (2½ fl oz/⅓ cup) extra virgin olive oil
130 g (4½ oz/½ cup) Greek or homemade yoghurt
  (page 216)
2 tablespoons salsa verde (page 217)
270 g (9½ oz/1½ cups) coarsely grated zucchini
100 g (3½ oz/1 cup) grated parmesan cheese
1 zucchini, cut into discs

Preheat the oven to 180°C/350°F. Grease a 21 x 11 cm (8½ x 4½ inch) loaf pan with melted butter.

Combine the flour, baking powder, pepper, salt, turmeric and goji berries in a mixing bowl. Using your hands, a whisk or the back of a spoon, break up any lumps and mix together well.

In another bowl, mix the eggs, olive oil, yoghurt, salsa verde, zucchini and parmesan together until evenly combined. Using a spatula, gently fold the dry ingredients into the wet mixture until the batter comes together.

Transfer batter to the prepared loaf pan. Arrange zucchini discs on top, slightly overlapping them like fish scales. Place in the oven and bake for 40–50 minutes, until golden on top and a skewer inserted into the centre of the loaf comes out clean.

Cool in the tin for 10 minutes, then turn out onto a wire rack to cool.

#LINEFORAWALK
#GILLCAMERON

BASICS

MILK
YOGHURT
MEAT FISH
EGGS FRUIT
GRAINS LEGUMES
VEGETABLES

HOMEMADE

Whenever anybody talks about homemade food I think of my grandma. She made everything from butter to preserves to even the best lamingtons in the state! If we were in my grandma's kitchen, I would be happy to say homemade always tastes better.

There is a simple reason why — and it's not just because she was an awesome cook. It's because she only used wholefood ingredients.

When you learn to make your own meals, you learn more about what you like, what makes things taste better, and how flavour is formed. But the real benefit of making your own homemade foods is the simple fact that you choose what goes into your body. (I have to admit, though, I sometimes order a pho master stock from my favourite Vietnamese place as it's almost impossible to recreate at home.)

We believe in eating real food that's been untainted by chemicals and hormones. Unfortunately, in the world we live, our everyday basic ingredients are increasingly becoming less and less pure and increasingly full of chemical additives, cheap filler and sugar to increase shelf life and profit margins.

The staples in this section are super simple recipes for flour, nut milks, cheese, butters and spreads, using real ingredients. In many cases they are so simple you'll wonder why we stopped making them at home and started buying them at all.

WHAT OILS TO USE

Not all oils are created equal. In fact, despite what has been common belief, some oils actually provide health benefits.

The healthiest oils and fats are the polyunsaturated ones, which include grapeseed and walnut oils. They contain omega-6 and omega-3, which lower the 'bad' LDL cholesterol and increase the 'good' HDL cholesterol. Monounsaturated fats are also good as they can help boost good cholesterol.

GRAPESEED OIL

High in polyunsaturated fats and vitamin E, this oil is one you can feel good about using. Grapeseed oil has a high smoke point, which makes it perfect for stir-frying and sautéing, and it's practically flavourless so your ingredients can be the star of the show.

WALNUT OIL

Unlike grapeseed oil, this has a low smoke point, so it doesn't perform well under heat, but its nutty flavour lends itself perfectly to salad dressings. It contains polyunsaturated fats, including alpha-linoleic acid (a heart-healthy, anti-inflammatory omega-3) and vitamin K, which can strengthen bones.

AVOCADO OIL

Avocado oil is high in monounsaturated fat, and lends a lovely flavour to vinaigrettes or drizzled over fish. Like other specialty oils, it can be on the pricey side, so refrigerate it to keep its subtle avocado flavour fresh, and bring it to room temperature before using.

COLD-PRESSED VIRGIN COCONUT OIL

Makes 1 cup

Before long, you'll be using this on everything – I know I do!

5 coconuts
5 cups water

Crack open the coconuts, remove the liquid (put it in the fridge to use later), and scrape out the coconut flesh using a spoon.

In batches, put the coconut flesh in a blender with the water and blend for 10 minutes, or until smooth. Transfer the mixture to a large bowl and using your hands, work and squeeze the pulp for about 20 minutes.

Strain the mixture into a large bowl lined with cheesecloth and squeeze out the liquid, reserving it in a jug. Repeat the straining and squeezing process 3 times, reserving all of the liquid (the pulp can be dehydrated and made into flour).

Pour the liquid into a jar with a large opening, cover with plastic wrap and set aside at room temperature for at least 48 hours.

Transfer to the fridge and refrigerate for 1 hour to help solidify the oil.

The solid layer on top is the oil; carefully scrape off this solid layer and store in an airtight container in the fridge until needed.

MILKS, NUTS, SEEDS & SPREADS

ACTIVATED NUTS
Makes 2 cups

Simply put, activated nuts are nuts that have been soaked in water for a period of time to activate the germination process. The nuts are then dehydrated at a low temperature.

Why activate nuts? It's claimed that activating them increases their nutritional value and helps with digestion. Nuts are full of great minerals like zinc, calcium and magnesium, as well as proteins and healthy fats, but raw, unactivated nuts have enzymes and phytic acid that inhibit absorption of all these goodies.

300 g (10½ oz/2 cups) nuts

Place nuts, 4 cups of water and a pinch of salt in a container and let them soak for at least 10 hours.

Preheat the oven or dehydrator to 85°C (185°F).

Strain the nuts, place them on a baking tray and leave in the oven for at least 15 hours. Make sure they are completely dehydrated, otherwise they will go mouldy.

Store in an airtight container for up to 2 weeks. They are ready to eat or can be used to make nut milk and butters.

SPROUTING SEEDS
Makes 1 cup

Sprouts are epic in raw salads and are great in tasty green smoothies and soups.

140 g (5 oz/1 cup) seeds or beans

Place the seeds or beans into a large mason jar, and fill the rest of the jar with warm filtered water and a pinch of sea salt. Cut a piece of cheesecloth or breathable mesh to size, and secure the cloth over the top of the jar with a rubber band. Leave to soak for at least 12 hours.

Without removing the cloth, rinse the seeds or beans by straining out the soaking water, then fill the jar with fresh water and give it a shake. Strain out the fresh water then turn the jar upside down and place in a sunny spot at an angle so that air can circulate, and the water can drain off.

Repeat this process at least twice daily. In 1 to 4 days, the sprouts will be ready. Rinse sprouts well, drain, and store in the jar (with the lid replaced) in the fridge.

Eat within 2 to 3 days.

HAZELNUT SPREAD
Makes 1–2 cups

2–3 cups hazelnuts roasted and skinned
1 teaspoon 100% raw cacao powder

Put the hazelnuts into a food processor and process for 20–30 minutes, stopping and scraping down the side as needed every five minutes. This takes more time than you'd expect, so be patient! The spread is ready when the oils have released from the nuts and it has a smooth consistency. Add the cacao and process to combine.

Transfer to a glass jar, seal and store in the fridge.

RAW NUT BUTTER
Makes 1–2 cups

Don't like dairy butter? Give this a try. You can use almost any nut, so get creative.

2–3 cups nuts of your choice, such as peanuts, hazelnuts, almonds, pistachios or cashews
1 teaspoon raw cacao (optional)

Put the nuts in a food processor and process for 20–30 minutes, stopping and scraping down the side as needed every 5 minutes. This takes more time than you'd expect, so be patient! It's ready when the oils have released from the nuts and the consistency is like smooth butter.

Stir in the raw cacao to make a delicious chocolate spread.

Transfer to a glass jar, seal and store in the fridge.

PEANUT BUTTER
Makes 1–2 cups

2–3 cups roasted unsalted peanuts

Put the peanuts into a food processor and process for

20–30 minutes, stopping and scraping down the side as needed every five minutes. This takes more time than you'd expect, so be patient! It's ready when the oils have released from the nuts and it has a smooth consistency.

Transfer to a glass jar, seal and store in the fridge.

COCONUT BUTTER
Makes 1 cup

This recipe only requires two ingredients: desiccated coconut, and a lot of patience. At first it will seem like the desiccated coconut will never turn into butter, but once the oil from the coconut starts to release, you'll get a smooth, velvety coconut butter, as if by magic. Trust us, it's worth the wait.

180–270 g (6–9½ oz/2–3 cups) desiccated coconut

Put the desiccated coconut in a high-speed blender and blend until it starts to form a smooth paste. This can take up to 15 minutes. Store in an airtight container in the fridge.

CULTURED BUTTER & BUTTERMILK
Makes 1 cup butter and 1 cup buttermilk

This butter has a zingy flavour and, for some people, the cultures can help with digestion.

500 ml (17 fl oz/2 cups) thin (pouring) cream
2 tablespoons cultured yoghurt

Start by making cultured cream. Put the cream in a small saucepan over medium heat and bring to the culturing temperature of 37.5°C (99.5°F). Remove the saucepan from the heat, add the cultured yoghurt and mix well.

If the saucepan has a tight-fitting lid, put that on. If not, transfer the mixture to a jar and screw the lid tight. Wrap the saucepan or jar in a warm towel or blanket and put in the warmest part of the house. Leave it there for 15–20 hours.

Transfer the saucepan or jar to the fridge to chill.

Put the cream in an electric mixer and, using the whisk attachment, mix for 10 minutes, or until the cream thickens, changes colour and starts to look like butter. Keep the mixer going past this point until suddenly the buttermilk drops out.

Using a strainer, strain the buttermilk off into a separate bowl, then use your hands to squeeze out any excess liquid. Place your butter into ice water to wash off any leftover buttermilk. Store the butter and buttermilk in airtight containers in the fridge.

COW'S BUTTER & BUTTERMILK
Makes 1 cup butter and 1 cup buttermilk

Butter has received a bit of a bad rap in the past, but good-quality unprocessed butter actually contains beneficial saturated fat, so it's a far better alternative to processed spreads such as margarine. When you make it yourself, you know exactly what's in it and what processes it went through to end up in your fridge. What's better than that?

500 ml (17 fl oz/2 cups) thin (pouring) cream

Put the cream in an electric mixer and, using the whisk attachment, mix for 10 minutes. The cream will thicken, then change colour to start to look like butter. Keep the mixer going past this point until suddenly the buttermilk drops out.

Using a strainer, strain the buttermilk into a separate bowl, then use your hands to squeeze out any leftover liquid from the butter.

To finish, put the butter into ice water to wash off any leftover buttermilk. Store the butter and buttermilk in airtight containers in the fridge.

If you want to infuse other flavours into the butter, such as thyme, truffle oil or garlic, simply add these at the beginning of the mixing process.

CHAI NUT MILK
Makes 1 litre (35 fl oz)

Delicious in smoothies!

1½ cups raw nuts of choice, such as almonds,
    macadamias or pistachios
1½ teaspoons chai leaves
1 vanilla bean, split and seeds scraped

Soak the nuts in water overnight. Strain and discard the water.

Brew chai tea with 1 litre (35 fl oz/4 cups) of hot water, chai leaves and vanilla, and let it steep for 5 minutes. Then strain the hot tea into a blender, and add the nuts.

Pulse to break up the nuts, then blend until all ingredients are liquid.

Strain through muslin or cheesecloth. Bottle and store in the fridge for up to 3 days.

HONEY VANILLA RICE MILK
Makes 1 litre (35 fl oz)

Make it at home so you know exactly what's gone in it – all the right goodies for all the right reasons.

2 cups cooked brown or white rice, or cooked quinoa
1 tablespoon honey
1 vanilla bean, split and seeds scraped

Put the rice or quinoa in a blender with 1.5 litres (52 fl oz/6 cups) water, honey and vanilla seeds.

Pulse to break up the rice or quinoa, and then blend until all ingredients are liquid.

Strain through muslin or cheesecloth. Bottle and store in the fridge for up to 3 days.

HEALTHY JAM
Makes 1½ cups

145 g (5 ½ oz/1 cup) mixed berries (frozen or fresh)
60 ml (2 fl oz/¼ cup) apple juice
1½ tablespoons chia seeds
1 tablespoon hemp seeds

1 tablespoon maple syrup
1 vanilla bean, split, seeds scraped
finely grated zest of 1 lemon
1 teaspoon finely grated fresh ginger
¼ teaspoon thyme leaves

Place the berries, apple juice, chia seeds, hemp seeds, maple syrup, vanilla seeds and lemon zest in a blender. Blend for about 30 seconds, just long enough to break up and combine everything.

Transfer mixture to a saucepan over medium heat, and add the ginger and thyme. Cook for 15–20 minutes, until jammy and reduced.

Store in an airtight container in the fridge for up to 3 weeks.

BREADS, GRAINS & SEEDS

SOURDOUGH STARTER

750 g (1 lb 11 oz) plain (all-purpose) flour (preferably organic - white, wholemeal or rye)

Day 1. In a large, non-reactive container (plastic or glass, not metal) mix together 150 g (5½ oz/1 cup) flour and 125 ml (4 fl oz/½ cup) water until combined and smooth. Cover the opening with some breathable cloth and secure with a rubber band or twine. Place on the kitchen bench out of direct sunlight and let sit for 24 hours to begin its fermentation process.

Day 2 (first feed). Have a look at the mixture – you might see a few little bubbles forming. This is good news as it means the wild yeast has started to work and form the starter. Remove and discard half the starter. Add 1 cup of flour and ½ cup of water and mix well. Re-cover the jar and place back on the kitchen bench for another 24 hours.

Day 3 (second feed). At this stage your starter should start to look active with some dotted bubbles on top, and should also be a thick and gluggy consistency when you mix it. Remove and discard half the starter. Add 1 cup of flour and ½ cup of water and mix well. Re-cover the jar and place back on the kitchen bench for another 24 hours.

Day 4 (third feed). The starter should have doubled in size and have large bubbles throughout. It should also have a pleasantly sweet and sour smell. Remove and discard half the starter. Add 1 cup of flour and ½ cup of water and mix well. Re-cover the jar and place back on the kitchen bench for another 24 hours.

Day 5. Once the starter is fluffy, bubbly and billowing, it is ready to use. If it's not there yet, don't stress – it just needs a few more days and feeds to get there. Just continue the feeding process until the starter is active.

When the starter is ready, use it as required in your chosen recipe, and continue to feed it every day. If you don't want to use your starter regularly, cover with a tight lid and refrigerate (this will slow down the fermentation). Feed your starter once a week and keep refrigerated. It will keep indefinitely in the fridge. Bring your starter out of the fridge at least 2 days before needing to use, feeding it for two cycles over that period to activate.

BENEFITS OF USING SOURDOUGH STARTER:

• **Taste** – It tastes amazing.

• **Digestion** – The fermenting bacteria + yeast combination helps to digest the starch in the flour.

• **Low gluten** – There are lower levels of gluten, as the gluten is transformed into amino acids during the long fermentation process.

• **Vitamins and minerals** – Lactic acid, produced during the fermentation process, makes the vitamins and minerals in the flour more available to the body. The integrity of sourdough is so complex that it contains a host of goodness in terms of nutrients. In sourdough, you can find vitamins B1-B6, B12, folate, thiamin, niacin, riboflavin, vitamin E, selenium, iron, manganese, calcium, magnesium, phosphorus, zinc and potassium.

• **Low GI** – Lactic acid slows down the release of glucose into the blood, giving sourdough a low GI (glycemic index) value. The sustained energy release of foods low in GI is believed to produce a more gradual rise in blood sugar and insulin levels in the body.

• **Longer shelf life** – The acid in the starter culture can delay firmness and staleness and prevent mould and bacterial spoilage.

NOTE

• The cooler the environment the longer your starter will take to become active, so be patient.

• The ideal room temperature is between 21–24°C (70–75°F).

WHY DISCARD STARTER?

• If you don't discard you'll eventually end up with a lot of sourdough starter.

• It keeps the ph balanced.

• It creates more food for the yeast cells, as they don't have to fight with so many other little yeast cells to get a feed.

BONDI HARVEST GRANOLA

Serves 5

This recipe is a mosh pit of goodness and it's so simple to make. I've always got granola handy in my pantry for a quick breakfast or a late-night guilt-free snack.

40 g (1½ oz/⅓ cup) rice bran
  (available from health or natural food stores)
30 g (1 oz/1 cup) puffed rice
100 g (3½ oz/¾ cup) sunflower seeds
225 g (8 oz/1¼ cup) roasted buckwheat
  (available from health or natural food stores)
75 g (2½ oz/⅓ cup) rolled amaranth
  (available from health or natural food stores)
30 g (1 oz/1 cup) puffed millet
  (available from health or natural food stores)
60 g (2 oz/½ cup) dried cranberries
90 g (3 oz/¾ cup) sultanas
90 g (3 oz/¾ cup) currants
40 g (1½ oz/¼ cup) goji berries
80 g (2¾ oz/½ cup) almonds
60 g (2 oz/¼ cup) banana chips
80 g (2¾ oz/⅔ cup) pepitas (pumpkin seeds)

Mix all the ingredients together in a bowl and transfer to an airtight container. Store in a cool dry place for up to 3 weeks.

HOW TO COOK MILLET

Makes 3 cups

Millet is a little like couscous, but it has the most wicked nutty flavour and it's gluten-free.

210 g (7½ oz/1 cup) millet
1 tablespoon coconut oil
500 ml (17 fl oz/2 cups) water or stock
1 whole garlic clove (optional)
1 red chilli, sliced in half (optional)
1 cinnamon stick (optional)

Run the millet under water for 5 minutes and drain in a fine mesh sieve.

Heat coconut oil in a medium saucepan over medium heat. Add the millet and toast until dry and golden (but not burnt) with a nutty taste and fragrance.

Add the water or stock and garlic, chilli and cinnamon, if using. Stir and bring to the boil. Reduce the heat to low and cook for 15 minutes, or until the liquid is absorbed.

Remove the saucepan from the heat and set aside for 10 minutes to finish cooking.

Remove the garlic, chilli and cinnamon, fluff the millet with a fork and serve.

TURMERIC FLATBREAD

Makes 5 breads

1½ teaspoons dried yeast
1 teaspoon sugar
260 g (9¼ oz/1 cup) natural or homemade yoghurt
  (page 216)
1 tablespoon ground turmeric
juice of ½ lemon
1 garlic clove, minced
pinch of sea salt
450 g (1 lb/3 cups) plain (all-purpose) flour, plus extra
  for dusting
3 teaspoons olive oil, plus extra for cooking

Combine yeast, sugar and 250 ml (9 fl oz/1 cup) warm water in a medium bowl. Stand for 5 minutes, until frothy.

In a separate bowl, combine the yoghurt, turmeric, juice, garlic and salt.

Place the flour in the bowl of an electric mixer and add the yeast mixture. Using a dough hook, slowly mix until the ingredients come together. Add the yoghurt mixture and continue mixing for 10-15 minutes, until it forms a springy dough. Add the olive oil just as it's finished mixing.

Transfer the dough to a large bowl and cover with a damp tea towel. Set aside for about 1 hour, until doubled in size.

Dust a clean work surface with extra flour. Turn out the

dough and divide into 5 portions. Roll out each portion to a long oval shape.

Heat a little oil in a large frying pan, or on a BBQ plate, over medium-high heat. Cook the dough for 6 minutes each side, until golden brown and bubbled.

TURMERIC QUINOA
Makes about 3 cups

190 g (6¾ oz/1 cup) quinoa
500 ml (17 fl oz/2 cups) stock or water
1 teaspoon turmeric (ground, or freshly grated)
1 sprig thyme, leaves picked (optional)
1 whole garlic clove (optional)

Place the quinoa into a fine sieve and rinse well under cold running water. Drain.

Heat the stock or water in a medium saucepan over medium heat. Add the quinoa, turmeric, thyme and garlic, if using.

Cover and bring to the boil. Turn heat to low and cook for 15 minutes, or until the quinoa becomes translucent. Remove the garlic before serving.

SAUCES, DIPS & CONDIMENTS

HOMEMADE YOGURT
Makes 4–5 cups

1 litre (34 fl oz/4 cups) whole milk
520 g (1 lb 2½ oz/2 cups) natural yoghurt
1 vanilla bean, split (optional)

Bring milk and vanilla bean to the boil in a heavy-based pot, then turn off heat. Let milk sit for 30 minutes until the heat reduces to 45°C (or until you can keep your finger in the milk).

Remove vanilla bean and then add yoghurt and whisk until well combined. Cover with foil or a lid and let sit at room temperature for 6–8 hours.

Transfer into an airtight container and place in the fridge. It will last up to a week.

YOGHURT TARTAR
Makes 600 ml (21 fl oz)

Using yoghurt instead of oils to make tartar sauce does three things: it lowers the fat content; gives it a zingy yoghurt tang; and also brings probiotic cultures into your diet. It's a win, win, win.

1 small handful parsley, leaves coarsely chopped
1 small handful coriander (cilantro),
  leaves coarsely chopped
250 g (9 oz) gherkins (pickles), coarsely chopped
1 tablespoon capers, drained and coarsely chopped
260 g (9¼ oz/1 cup) Greek or homemade yoghurt
  (see above)
1 tablespoon dijon mustard
juice of 1 lemon

Put all of the ingredients in a large jar and mix well. Season with salt and pepper and store in the fridge in an airtight container.

HOLLANDAISE SAUCE
Serves 2–3

Want to really impress someone with breakfast in bed? Then this is a must.

3 egg yolks
2 tablespoons apple cider vinegar
juice of 1 lemon
175 g (6 oz) 'grass-fed' butter, diced

Half-fill a medium saucepan with water and bring to a simmer over medium heat.

Put the egg yolks, vinegar and lemon juice in a heatproof bowl that will fit over the saucepan.

Place the bowl over the simmering saucepan to create a double-boiler and, using a whisk, whisk the mixture continuously for 5 minutes, until light ribbons begin to form. Add the butter one cube at a time, whisking to incorporate each one, and keeping the water at a light simmer.

Once all the butter is incorporated, season with salt and pepper and serve immediately.

TIP: Once you've mastered this basic recipe, feel free to make it your own and try some different flavours. To the finished sauce you could add:

- shaved truffles or ½ teaspoon truffle oil
- juice and rind of 1 orange
- or ½ teaspoon wasabi purée.

AÏOLI
Makes 1 litre (35 fl oz)

You can do it with a machine or whisk it by hand, but you've got to know how to make a great aïoli.

1 head of garlic
1 litre (35 fl oz/4 cups) olive oil, plus extra
  for roasting garlic
3 eggs
3 egg yolks, extra
1 tablespoon dijon mustard
1 tablespoon white wine vinegar

To roast the garlic, preheat the oven to 180°C (350°F). Toss the garlic in olive oil, put on a baking tray lined with baking paper and cook for 15–20 minutes, until soft. Allow to cool, then squeeze the garlic flesh into a small bowl.

METHOD 1: Put the eggs, extra egg yolks, mustard, vinegar and 1 tablespoon of the roasted garlic in a food processor or blender. Start the motor, then slowly drizzle in the oil. Season with salt and pepper to taste.

METHOD 2: Put the eggs, extra egg yolks, mustard, vinegar and 1 tablespoon of the roasted garlic in a large bowl. Combine using a whisk, then start drizzling in the oil very slowly, whisking continuously, until the aïoli is thick and creamy. Season with salt and pepper to taste.

GUACAMOLE
Serves 4

Everyone's super Mexican friend. Served with tacos or just some corn chips, there's always space for guac on my table.

1 avocado
1 large handful coriander (cilantro), leaves chopped
juice of 1 lime
juice of 1 lemon
½ garlic clove, minced

Put all ingredients in a medium bowl and mash like it's a mosh pit. Season with salt and pepper and dig in.

SALSA VERDE
Makes 1 cup

Salsa verde literally means 'green sauce'. It's zesty and herbaceous and goes perfectly with any seafood.

1 spring onion (scallion), diced
½ cup chopped parsley
½ cup chopped mint
½ cup chopped basil
½ tablespoon dijon mustard
½ tablespoon capers, drained and finely chopped
100 ml (3½ fl oz) extra virgin olive oil
3 anchovies, diced
1 garlic clove, minced

Combine all ingredients in a medium bowl. Season with salt and pepper to taste and store in an airtight container in the fridge.

SMOKY CHILLI JAM
Makes 2 cups

This takes a bit of time, but it's well worth the effort. Once you've tried this, you'll turn up your nose to any other chilli sauce that comes your way.

250 ml (9 fl oz/1 cup) coconut oil
1 onion, diced
4 garlic cloves, minced
1 teaspoon smoked paprika
1 cm (½ inch) piece fresh ginger, chopped
1½ red capsicums (peppers), charred,
   skin removed and diced
3 red chillies, charred, skin removed and diced
   (keep the seeds)
175 g (6 oz) tinned tomatoes
175 g (6 oz) palm sugar (jaggery)
200 ml (7 fl oz) fish or chicken stock (pages 220-221)

Heat coconut oil in a large saucepan or stockpot over medium heat. Add the onion, garlic, paprika, ginger, capsicum, chilli, tomato and palm sugar and cook for about 10–15 minutes, or until caramelised and collapsed. Add the stock and cook for 10 minutes. Set aside to cool.

Purée the mixture in a blender in batches. Store the jam in an airtight 500 ml (17 fl oz/2 cups) container.

KALE PESTO
Makes 300ml (10½ fl oz)

This is definitely not a traditional pesto, but it's just as tasty. The addition of kale not only ups the hipster level but the health benefits too, and the almonds add flavour and oils.

1 garlic clove
200 ml (7 fl oz) olive oil
3 pinches of sea salt flakes
½ cup picked basil leaves
½ cup finely chopped kale leaves
½ cup toasted almonds
zest and juice of ½ lemon
½ cup finely grated parmesan cheese

We like to use a mortar and pestle to make our pesto. Put the garlic with a little of the olive oil and a pinch of sea salt in the mortar (bowl). Push with the pestle to break up the garlic until you have a paste.

Add the basil, a little more olive oil and another pinch of sea salt. Grind the basil with the pestle to break it down to a paste. Repeat with the kale.

Add the almonds and break up a little with the pestle.

Add the lemon zest and juice, and the parmesan cheese and pound with the pestle to get a pesto consistency.

Store in an airtight container in the fridge.

BASIC TOMATO SAUCE
Makes 2–3 cups

60 ml (2 fl oz/¼ cup) olive oil
4 garlic cloves, minced
1 red chilli, minced (keep the seeds if you like it hot)
3 onions, diced
500 g (1 lb 2 oz) tinned diced tomatoes
1 tablespoon fresh oregano leaves

Heat the olive oil in a large heavy-based saucepan over medium heat. Add the garlic, chilli and onion and cook until the onion is tender. Add the tomato, reduce the heat to low and cook for 1 hour. Season with salt and pepper to taste. Remove from the heat.

Put the sauce in a blender and blend in batches. Stir through the oregano and serve with pasta or use as a base for other recipes.

HOMEMADE TAHINI
Makes ⅓ cup

Used in several recipes throughout this book, this tahini's also fab on toast with honey and banana.

145 g (5 oz/1 cup) sesame seeds, toasted
1½ tablespoons sesame oil

Put the sesame seeds in a food processor and process for 20–30 minutes, stopping and scraping down the side as needed every 5 minutes.

Add the sesame oil and salt to taste, if you like, and process until a smooth paste forms.

Transfer to a glass jar, seal and store in the fridge.

HUMMUS
Makes 3 cups

500 g (1 lb 2 oz) cooked chickpeas
2 garlic cloves, minced
200 ml (7 fl oz) olive oil
finely grated zest and juice of 2 lemons
2 teaspoons ground cumin
½ teaspoon ground cinnamon

Place all the ingredients into a food processor or blender with 2 tablespoons cold water. Process until smooth, then season with salt and pepper.

To make pesto hummus, add 2 tablespoons homemade pesto (page 126).

To make pumpkin hummus, add 4 tablespoons pumpkin purée.

Store in an airtight container in the fridge for up to 1 week.

PISTACHIO DUKKAH
Makes 4 cups

280 g (10 oz/2 cups) shelled pistachios
225 g (8 oz/1½ cups) sesame seeds
2 tablespoons ground coriander
2 tablespoons ground cumin
35 g (1¼ oz/½ cup) shredded coconut
finely grated zest of 2 lemons
1 tablespoon ground black pepper
2 teaspoons sea salt

Preheat oven to 200°C (400°F) and line a baking tray with baking paper.

Mix all the ingredients together, and spread evenly onto the prepared tray. Bake for 15 minutes, until toasted, then set aside to cool.

Store in an airtight container for up to 2 weeks.

INFUSED SALTS & RUBS

Infused salts are a great and easy way to add attitude to your cooking, curing and seasoning.

GRAVLAX SALT RUB
Makes 2 cups

Rub this over a salmon fillet, let it sit in the fridge overnight and BAM! – gravlax salmon done.

1 tablespoon black peppercorns, toasted
220 g (7¾ oz/1 cup) sugar
290 g (10¼ oz/1 cup) salt
2 tablespoons fennel seeds, toasted
finely grated zest of 2 lemons
finely grated zest of 1 orange
finely grated zest of 1 lime

Put the black peppercorns in the bowl of a mortar and break up well using the pestle. Add the other ingredients and grind gently to mix. Store in an airtight container.

BONDI HARVEST BASIC SALT RUB
Makes 2 cups

580 g (20½ oz/2 cups) salt
2 sprigs thyme
2 sprigs rosemary
2 bay leaves
4 tablespoons black pepper
4 tablespoons fennel seeds

Combine all ingredients in a medium-sized bowl and store in an airtight container.

CITRUS SALT
Makes 1 cup

290 g (10¼ oz/1 cup) salt
finely grated zest of 1 lemon
finely grated zest of 1 lime
finely grated zest of 1 orange

Combine all ingredients in a medium bowl and store in an airtight container.

CHILLI PEPPER SALT
Makes 1 cup

½ tablespoon black peppercorns, toasted
4 red chillies, halved, seeded
290 g (10¼ oz/1 cup) salt

Break up the peppercorns using a mortar and pestle. Put the chillies and salt in a bowl, add the peppercorns and mix well. Store in an airtight container.

SESAME SALT
Makes 1 cup

300 g (10½ oz/2 cups) unhulled sesame seeds
1 teaspoon garlic powder
½ teaspoon dried chilli flakes
30 g (1 oz/¼ cup) sea salt

To make the sesame salt, toast the sesame seeds in a dry frying pan until golden. Cool slightly. Use a mortar and pestle or spice blender to grind the seeds, garlic powder, chilli and salt to a medium-coarse powder. Store in an airtight container.

PASTRAMI MEAT RUB
Makes 1 cup

Make this up and have it handy in your pantry and, I'm telling you, you'll never want to barbeque meat without it again.

1 tablespoon garlic powder
1 tablespoon ground coriander
3 tablespoons smoked paprika
1 tablespoon dark brown sugar
5 tablespoons black peppercorns, toasted
4 tablespoons sea salt

Put all the ingredients in a mortar and break up using the pestle. Pound and grind for 5 minutes, or until a coarse consistency. Store in an airtight container.

STOCKS

CHICKEN STOCK
Makes about 3 litres (105 fl oz/12 cups)

Chicken stock's my go-to stock for risottos, as it's full-flavoured without being overpowering.

2 chicken carcasses
1 onion, chopped
2 garlic cloves, chopped
2 red chillies, chopped (keep the seeds)
4 celery sticks, chopped
2 carrots, chopped
3 bay leaves
2 sprigs rosemary
4 black peppercorns

Place all the ingredients in a large saucepan with 5 litres (170 fl oz/20 cups) water over high heat. Bring to the boil, reduce the heat to a simmer and cook uncovered for 2–3 hours.

Ladle the fat from the surface of the stock. Strain through a fine strainer or muslin. Allow to cool to room temperature and refrigerate in an airtight container for up to 5 days or freeze for up to 4 months.

BEEF STOCK
Makes about 3 litres (105 fl oz/12 cups)

Or, if you're hipster, bone broth. Beef stock/bone broth is ridiculously good for you and super cheap. Make a big batch and freeze it, and you'll always be ready for a cold rainy night.

2 kg (4 lb 8 oz) beef bones, chopped into 5 cm (2 inch) pieces
150 ml (5 fl oz) olive oil
2 onions, chopped
1 head of garlic, halved
2 carrots, chopped
2 celery sticks, chopped
90 g (3¼ oz/1 cup) chopped mushrooms
6 parsley stalks
4 black peppercorns
2 sprigs thyme
2 sprigs rosemary
4 bay leaves

Preheat the oven to 180°C (350°F). Put the beef bones in a roasting tray and roast for 5–8 minutes, until golden.

Meanwhile, heat the olive oil in a stockpot or large saucepan over medium-high heat. Add the onion, garlic, carrot, celery and mushroom and cook until tender and slightly coloured.

Add the roasted bones, parsley stalks, black peppercorns, thyme, rosemary, bay leaves and 8 litres (270 fl oz/32 cups) water and increase the heat to high. Bring to the boil (this should take about 10 minutes), skimming the fats and impurities the whole time, then reduce the heat to a light simmer and cook uncovered for 4 hours, skimming the surface every 30 minutes.

Strain the stock through a fine strainer or muslin. Allow to cool and store in an airtight container in the fridge for up to 3 days or in the freezer for up to 3 months.

VEGETABLE STOCK
Makes about 3 litres (105 fl oz/12 cups)

This stock is so simple and adds loads of flavour and extra nutrients when cooking quinoa and grains.

1 head of garlic, halved
500 g (1 lb 2 oz) mushrooms, chopped
3 celery sticks, chopped
3 onions, chopped
3 carrots, chopped
7 parsley stalks
4 black peppercorns
3 sprigs thyme
2 sprigs rosemary
4 bay leaves

Put all the ingredients in a stockpot or large saucepan with 5 litres (170 fl oz/20 cups) water over medium heat. Cook uncovered for 2–3 hours at a simmer.

Strain the stock through a fine strainer or muslin cloth. Allow to cool and store in an airtight container in the fridge for up to 3 days or freeze for up to 3 months.

SHELLFISH BROTH
Makes about 3 litres (105 fl oz/12 cups)

'Never waste anything' is what you get taught in a professional kitchen. Just freeze your prawn shells and fish skeletons and, when you have enough, pull them out and boom – shellfish broth city.

2 kg (4 lb 8 oz) fish bones and heads, chopped, and shellfish shells
2½ tablespoons olive oil
1 garlic clove, chopped
1 onion, sliced
1 leek, white part only, sliced
2 celery sticks, sliced
½ fennel bulb, sliced
1 tablespoon tomato paste (concentrated purée)
3 tomatoes, diced
250 ml (9 fl oz/1 cup) white wine
pinch of saffron
4 bay leaves
1 sprig thyme
1 sprig rosemary
6 parsley stalks

Clean the fish bones and shellfish shells with running water, washing away any blood and discarding all innards.

Heat the oil in a stock pot or large saucepan over medium heat. Add the garlic, onion, leek, celery and fennel and sweat for 10 minutes, or until the vegetables are soft but not coloured. Add the fish bones and shellfish shells and cook for 5 minutes. Add the tomato paste, tomato, wine and saffron and cook for 5 minutes, or until reduced by half.

Add 4 litres (135 fl oz/16 cups) water, bay leaves, thyme, rosemary and parsley stalks, and simmer uncovered for 20–30 minutes. Don't allow the stock to boil or it will become cloudy.

Strain through a fine strainer or muslin. Allow to cool and store in an airtight container in the fridge for up to 3 days or in the freezer for up to 3 months.

FISH STOCK
Makes about 3 litres (105 fl oz/12 cups)

I catch a lot of fish and, out of respect, I make sure I use the whole fish, including the bones. Fish stock is a great way to use the bones.

2 kg (4 lb 8 oz) fish bones, chopped
2½ tablespoons olive oil
1 garlic clove, chopped
1 onion, sliced
1 leek, white part only, sliced
2 celery sticks, sliced
½ fennel bulb, sliced
250 ml (9 fl oz/1 cup) white wine
4 bay leaves
1 sprig thyme
1 sprig rosemary
6 parsley stalks

Clean the fish bones with running water, washing away any blood and discarding all innards.

Heat the oil in a stockpot or large saucepan over medium heat. Add the garlic, onion, leek, celery and fennel and sweat for 10 minutes, or until the vegetables are soft but not coloured. Add the fish bones and cook for 5 minutes. Add the wine and cook for 5 minutes, or until reduced by half.

Add 4 litres (135 fl oz/16 cups) water, bay leaves, thyme, rosemary and parsley stalks and simmer uncovered for 20–30 minutes. Don't allow the stock to boil or it will become cloudy.

Strain through a fine strainer or muslin. Allow to cool and store in an airtight container in the fridge for up to 3 days or in the freezer for up to 3 months.

FOOD STORAGE

How good is it when you start to see the new-season fruits and veg at the markets or grocer? Recipes and treats you've been thinking about since this time last year are suddenly back on the menu!

Then, how often do you cram your bought goodies into your tote only to get them home and find you have bruised or damaged your spoils in the hurry home!

The first lesson in any professional kitchen is to love and respect your produce. Then, it'll return the favour with long life, nutrition and flavour for days.

In this section, I teach you a few simple tricks and tips I have picked up along the way for proper care and storage of your produce so it tastes better for longer. A lot is actually common sense, of course — like maybe packing your produce in a box to carry home.

SAFE STORAGE TEMPERATURES

Fridge Temp 4° C (40° F)

Freezer Temp -18° C (0° F)

When freezing food, most people make the mistake of not sealing it in an airtight container or freezer bag before placing it in the freezer. Food not properly sealed will get that awful freezer burn from the cold air and dry out.

Dry Storage (Pantry) Temp 10°C (50°F) to 20°C (70°F)

The basic rule here is always: the cooler the better. Also remember to keep your dry store away from direct sunlight, in a dry, clean and well-ventilated pantry.

FOOD ROTATION & FIFO

Don't you hate it when you find that the great produce you bought last week and placed in your fridge crisper has turned into a mushy, gross mess?

To stop that from happening, all you've gotta do is apply one simple rule. When unpacking new produce and ingredients, always bring the older produce to the front and place the new in the back. At Bondi Harvest Restaurant we use the acronym FIFO (see below) to help remind the kitchen staff of this process. Food Rotation applies to the fridge, freezer and dry store, and is the key to keeping track of the freshness of your produce and cutting down on waste.

F - First

I - In

F - First

O - Out

VEGETABLES & FRUIT

It's always worth spending that little bit more time and love on unpacking your produce properly. Storing your fruit and vegetables correctly will not only make them last a lot longer but will also make them tastier — and at the end of the day, that's what I'm after.

The biggest piece of advice I can give is to be gentle, have some respect for the ingredients, and treat them with some love and care. Scratching, bruising and damaging fresh produce can break the cell walls, speeding up oxidation and the spoiling process.

Don't stack. Try to store ingredients in single layers and, if you absolutely have to, make sure heavy and more hardy items are at the base and the delicates are on top.

DO NOT REFRIGERATE :

Vegetables (whole) - cucumbers, eggplant, garlic, ginger, onions, potatoes, pumpkin, sweet potato, tomatoes.

Fruit (whole) - avocados, apples, bananas, citrus, melons, mangos, persimmons, pomegranates, watermelon.

REFRIGERATE:

Vegetables - artichokes, asparagus, beets, Belgian endive, broccoli, Brussel sprouts, cabbage carrots, cauliflower, celery, green beans, leeks, mushrooms, peas, radishes, summer squashes, sweet corn, + cut, ripe and overripe vegetables.

Fruit - apples (more than 1 week), apricots, Asian pears berries, cherries, figs, grapes, + cut, ripe and overripe fruit.

HERBS & SALADS

Using fresh herbs and salad in a dish is such a simple way to elevate the simplest of dishes and add a heap of extra flavour. When shopping for herbs and salads, choose the bunches with the root still attached. These bunches are still alive, and will last longer and even continue to grow if you store them properly and give them the love they deserve.

Herbs are sorted into two categories: soft and hard. Soft herbs are usually more delicate and palatable, like parsley, coriander, mint and dill. Hard herbs usually have a woodier stalk, are strongly fragrant and have more essential oils, like rosemary, thyme, oregano and marjoram.

SOFT HERBS

Store fresh soft herbs as you would flowers. If they have roots, leave them on; if not, just snip off their bases and pop them in a jar of water on the kitchen counter. If it's a hot day, place the whole jar in the fridge. Pluck off what you need when you need it and change the water daily.

Revive wilted herbs, or get back the crunch in veggies like celery and carrots, by putting them in a bowl of iced water.

HARD HERBS

Store fresh hard herbs by wrapping them first in damp paper or a tea towel, then in plastic wrap or an airtight container in the fridge.

Dry: if you have an excess of hard herbs, drying them for later use is super simple. All you need to do is hang them from their stems and keep them in a cool, dry and well-ventilated area for at least a week until they dehydrate and crumble off their stems.

Herb Salt: preheat your oven to 100-120°C then place your herbs onto a baking tray with baking paper, spreading them out into an even layer. Sprinkle with just enough salt to cover and bake overnight until they're dry. Place them in a processor and blend until powdered. Store in an airtight container for seasoning and curing.

SALAD WITH ROOT

As with soft herbs, just pop them in a jar of water on the kitchen counter. If it's a hot day, place the whole jar in the fridge. Pluck off what you need and change the water daily.

LOOSE SALAD

The first thing I like to do is remove the loose salad mix from its plastic and pick through it. I discard any discoloured or bruised leaves, as these will turn quickest and spoil the rest of the salad. I then line a plastic storage container with paper towels and add the greens on top. Then I just cover this with another layer of paper towels and store the salad in the fridge.

When it comes to meat, poultry and seafood we believe in making consensus choices to only buy and support quality organic, local and free-range farmers and suppliers. Consciously sourcing organic, local and free-range ingredients supports our farmers, and the produce tastes 1000 times better. It's not just better for you but also for mother nature and the environment.

MEAT & POULTRY PURCHASING TIPS

RELATIONSHIP

· Talk to and build a relationship with your butcher.

SIZE

· Bigger isn't always better. Look for flavour not size.

WHOLE ANIMALS

· There's way too much wastage in this world. Buy meat from a butcher that does whole-animal butchery. Support professionals who support the environment and whole-animal usage.

- Try to buy whole poultry. You get a lot more for your money, and the bones and carcass are perfect for making stocks, sauces and soups.

COLOUR

- Keep in mind that with pork, beef, lamb, veal, etc., red is the colour of freshness. Simply put, the redder the meat, the fresher it is.

STORAGE

- **Refrigerate** - Always store meat and poultry separately in airtight containers or on a tray to ensure that juices do not leak onto other food items. Store on the bottom shelf of the fridge and never store cooked and raw meat together.

- **Freeze** - Re-wrap meat and poultry products tightly and label with the date before freezing. Use freezer paper or plastic freezer bags to prevent freezer burn affecting your produce.

- **Defrost** - Defrost produce in the fridge overnight on a tray or inside a plastic storage container to ensure that juices do not leak onto other food items.

SEAFOOD PURCHASING TIPS

SUSTAINABLE

Choosing sustainable fish can be confusing, so here are some tips to make it a little bit easier:

- Choose line- and pole-caught fish
- Talk to your fish supplier
- Choose local
- Buy whole fish
- Do some research and educate yourself on sustainable species

LOCAL

- Whenever possible choose local, not imported, seafood. Fish that has been caught locally has spent less time in transit, supports local fisherman, and will be fresher and better for the environment.

WHOLE FISH

- Where possible choose whole fish. You'll get more for your money and the bones are perfect for making stocks and soups. If you're not confident filleting, ask your supplier to do it for you.

FIRM

- Skin and flesh should be taut, clean and glistening, almost as if the fish were still alive. If the skin is sunken, soft and mushy, pick something else.

RED GILLS

- One of the best indicators of freshness is bright red-coloured gills; if they're discoloured or grey, choose again.

CLEAR EYES

- Fish eyes don't lie and are a great indicator of freshness. Look for clear, bright, colourful and convex eyes. If the eyes are cloudy, sunken and discoloured, then select another fish.

SMELL

- Fresh fish should smell salty and like the sea. If it has a strong odour, pick another fish.

STORAGE

- **Refrigerate** - Scale, clean, gut and wipe down with clean paper towel. Place it on a clean plate or tray or in a lidded container. Cover with plastic wrap or the lid. Store in the coldest part of the fridge and use within 3 days.

- **Freeze** - Scale, clean, gut and wipe down with clean paper towel. Place in an airtight freezer bag and extract as much air as possible from the bag before sealing it. Date, label and freeze.

- **Defrost** - Defrost produce in the fridge overnight on a tray or inside a plastic storage container to ensure that juices do not leak onto other food items.

About the Authors

GUY TURLAND

With his roots in Bowral, Guy moved to Bondi in 2003 to undertake his chef's apprenticeship. Upon finishing, he was snapped up by some of Sydney's top kitchens, including Est., which won Restaurant of the Year in Guy's first year working there. A common love of surfing and food saw chef Peter Doyle personally mentor Guy and, under his guidance, Guy learned all aspects of the kitchen. Every chef has a career-defining experience and this was his. In 2007 Guy moved on to Bondi Icebergs, attracted by chef Robert Marchetti's simple, respectful approach to Italian cooking.

In March of the same year Guy bought a run-down café in North Bondi, now Jo and Willy's Depot, where he maintains creative control of the kitchen and continues to fine-tune his own food style. A keen free diver, Guy and his mates dive most weeks and know where and when the fish are plentiful in Bondi's fertile waters. Always respectful of the sustainable catch, the boys are often seen carrying lobsters or kingfish as long as your arm home for a cook-up with friends.

In 2014 Guy opened his first Bondi Harvest café in Bondi Junction, offering a local, seasonal and healthy wholefood-inspired menu. Later that year he published his first cookbook *Bondi Harvest* with HarperCollins, now selling in USA and the UK as well as in Australia.

In 2016 Guy spent six months in California, expanding the brand in the USA. During that time, he renovated and opened his second café, Bondi Harvest Santa Monica.

2017 sees a second Bondi Harvest café in USA and a flagship Bondi Harvest TV show.

MARK ALSTON

Husband and father of two, Mark grew up running amok on his family farm outside Wagga Wagga in the Riverina. Initially it looked as though farming was his clear trajectory, having enrolled in a science degree at university, but after volunteering on student films at the Australian Film Television and Radio School, Mark found his true passion.

Mark started his career loading film in camera departments and working on feature film productions which included *The Matrix 2* & *3*, *Star Wars*, *The Last Samurai*, *Superman* and *Narnia*. After working solidly on US features for 5 years it was time for a change.

Mark learned story in the editing department, then quickly moved into directing. He was soon nominated for an ARIA for Best Music Video. After a number of years directing advertising (and winning a Bronze Lion along the way), Mark again needed a change of scene – he attended AWARD school. Armed with a renewed outlook on creative thinking and idea generation, he moved towards the development of new digital formats.

A yearning to connect again with farming and food saw Mark establish Bondi Harvest with Guy Turland in 2013. Mark now combines his passion for food and the environment with that of photography and film-making through Bondi Harvest.

Acknowledgements

GUY

From the end of an era to new generations and into the future, I have so much to be thankful for. No words will ever give weight to how grateful and honoured I am to have so many supportive and inspiring people in my life.

Mark: what a journey, mate! I hope you know how grateful I am for all the hard work, loyalty and creativity you've put into making this happen. Loosie, Eddie and Sunny: thanks for lending me this great man to enable us to build something amazing together.

Family. Mum and Dad: your guidance, support and love give me the strength to take opportunities and to chase my goals. You've taught me to be humble, hungry and loving; you're a constant inspiration to me. Cade, Clint, Miranda, Carli, Dave: having siblings is like having built-in best friends; you've shaped me in every way and it's an honour to have you close.

Vali + Luna: you fill my world with a sense of wonder and excitement; I strive to make a difference in this world for you.

To my late grandfather 'Farmy' and beautiful grandmother 'Nan': my spark and love for food comes from you. You've shaped me into the man I am today – from porridge, pies and love-heart sponge cakes, you're always in my heart.

Erin: forever my partner in adventure and life, you're my rock ! Your patience, understanding and love have given me the strength to share my passion with the world.

To the team at Harper Collins – Catherine, Lisa, Madeleine and Lu – and Rob Palmer and Deb Kaloper: thanks for believing in us. We're so proud to have created this gorgeous book with such a talented group of people.

Sabrina and Dave: I hope you know how much we appreciate your hard work, dedication and loyalty. Tony, Lupita, Shirley, Martin, Vanessa: you're the beating heart of the café; so excited to grow with you.

MARK

It's such a privilege to be able to publish our second Bondi Harvest cookbook. Never in my wildest dreams could I have imagined where this little side project could have taken us. Of course, there are a few people I need to thank for their work on this book, their work on Bondi Harvest and for continued support.

I would like to thank my family, and in particular, Loosie, Eddie and Sunny for being the foundation upon which this is all built – I hope I can be as solid a footing for you as you are for me.

I would like to thank Catherine, Lisa, Rob, Deb, Madeleine and Lu for your help in pulling this book together.

I would also like to thank Dean, Kevin, Anna and Sara for your work on all things Bondi Harvest. Without you guys most of our improbable dreams could not be realised.

To the team at Bondi Harvest, Santa Monica – you guys are the best! Sabrina, Dave, Shirley, Vanessa, Lupita, Tony, Carlos, Martin and everyone else. You are the heart and the smile of Bondi Harvest day in and day out. Thank you – you guys rock.

Lastly, I would like to thank Guy. Mate, we have come a long way but I am constantly in awe of your focus and talents. It has been a wonderful few years working with you and becoming even better mates. Yew!

INDEX

HarperCollinsPublishers

First published in Australia in 2017
by HarperCollinsPublishers Australia Pty Limited
ABN 36 009 913 517
harpercollins.com.au

HarperCollinsPublishers

Level 13, 201 Elizabeth Street, Sydney NSW 2000, Australia
Unit D1, 63 Apollo Drive, Rosedale, Auckland 0632, New Zealand
A 53, Sector 57, Noida, UP, India
1 London Bridge Street, London, SE1 9GF, United Kingdom
2 Bloor Street East, 20th floor, Toronto, Ontario M4W 1A8, Canada
195 Broadway, New York NY 10007, USA

ISBN 978 0 7322 9987 3

Cover and internal photography by Rob Palmer
Styling by Deb Kaloper
Cover and internal design by Lisa White
Internal illustrations by Daniel Giscard Hernandez/Lisa White
Photographs on pages 12–15, 52, 139, 166, 176, 182, 200 © Mark Alston
Props courtesy of Belinda Tee Ceramics/MH Ceramics/The Establishment Studios
With thanks to the Bondi Harvest community taking part in the photographic stories
Colour reproduction by Graphic Print Group, South Australia
Printed and bound in China by RR Donnelley

8 7 6 5 4 3 2 1   17 18 19 20 21